Owning It All

Essays by

William Kittredge

Graywolf Press

SAINT PAUL, MINNESOTA

Publication of this volume is made possible in part by a grant provided by the Minnesota State Arts Board, through an appropriation by the Minnesota State Legislature, a grant from the Wells Fargo Foundation Minnesota, and a grant from the National Endowment for the Arts. Significant support has also been provided by the Bush Foundation; the Lannan Foundation; Marshall Field's Project Imagine with support from the Target Foundation; the McKnight Foundation; and other generous contributions from foundations, corporations, and individuals. To these organizations and individuals we offer our heartfelt thanks.

The essays in this collection have been considerably revised since their first appearance in the following periodicals: *Rocky Mountain Magazine, Outside, Montana: The Magazine of Western History, American West, The Movies, Dial, Pacific Northwest,* and *Northern Lights.*

Published by Graywolf Press
2402 University Avenue, Suite 203
Saint Paul, Minnesota 55114
All rights reserved.

www.graywolfpress.org

Published in the United States of America

ISBN 1-55597-366-3

2   4   6   8   9   7   5   3   1

Library of Congress Control Number: 2001096560

Cover design: VetoDesignUSA.com
Cover photograph: ©2002 PhotoDisc, Inc.

Contents

For Annick

Owning It All

Home

IN THE LONG-AGO LAND of my childhood we clearly understood the high desert country of southeastern Oregon as the actual world. The rest of creation was distant as news on the radio.

In 1945, the summer I turned thirteen, my grandfather sentenced his chuckwagon cow outfit to a month of haying on the IXL, a little ranch he had leased from the Sheldon Antelope Refuge in Nevada. Along in August we came in to lunch one noontime and found the cook, a woman named Hannah, flabbergasted by news that some bomb had just blown up a whole city in Japan. Everybody figured she had been into the vanilla extract, a frailty of cooks in those days. As we know, it was no joke. Nagasaki and then VJ Day. We all listened to that radio. Great changes and possibilities floated and cut in the air. But such far-off strange events remained the concern of people who lived in cities. We might get drunk and celebrate, but we knew such news really had nothing to do with us. Not in the far outback of southeastern Oregon.

When I came home from the Air Force in 1958, I found our backland country rich with television from the Great World. But that old attitude from my childhood, the notion that my people live in a separate kingdom where they own it all, secure from the world, is still powerful and troublesome. When people ask where I'm from I still say southeastern Oregon, expecting them to understand my obvious pride.

JACK RAY WAS ONE of the heroes of my boyhood. A slope-shouldered balding little man, Jack dominated the late roughhouse craziness at our mid-July country dances. The Harvest Moon Ball.

"He can hit like a mule kicking," my father used to say after those dances, winking at us kids and grinning at my mother's back while she served up a very late Sunday breakfast of steak and fried mush and biscuits and thick sausage gravy.

At that time I was maybe five or six years old, and I would have been asleep in the backseat of our car for a couple of hours when the shouting and fighting started around midnight. So I recall those scenes with a newly awakened child's kind of strobe-light clarity, a flash here and there, all illuminated in the headlights of 1930s automobiles. The ranch women would be crowded outside onto the porch where they could see, some wife weeping, the men out closer to the battle in the parking lot, passing bottles.

But what I see mainly is Jack Ray getting up off the ground, wiping a little trickle of blood from the corner of his mouth, glancing down at the smear on his hand, his eyes gone hard while some sweating farm boy moved at him again; and torn shirts, the little puffs of dust their feet kicked there in the headlights. At that point my memory goes fragile. There is some quick slippery violence, and the farm boy is on his knees. Jack Ray is standing above him, waiting, wheezing as he breathes.

It's over, everybody knows, and soon it is. Two more grunting punches, and the farm boy is down again, and Jack Ray steps back, his eyes gone soft and almost bewildered in the light as a little shudder moves through the crowd, and someone shouts, and the bottles pass again. I see Jack Ray, there in those headlights, smiling like a child now that it's finished, the farm boy up on his knees, shaking his head.

No harm done, the air clear. I see it over and over, summer dance after summer dance. I see the kind of heroism
my boyhood educated me to understand and respect.

And I hate the part that comes next. I grew up and ran
the haying and combine crews on our ranch, and there
eventually came a time when I hired Jack Ray to work for
me. He had worked a lot of seasons for my father, and such
men always had a job with us. Jack was maybe fifty by that
time and crippled by his life, the magic gone, a peaceable
man who seemed to have turned a little simple. He did what
he could, chores around the cookhouse, and once in a while
he drank. After a bout in town that earned him some time
in the county jail, he would show up grinning in the
bunkhouse.

"Well, hell, Jack," I would say, "it's a new day."

"Kid," he would say, "she's a new world every morning."

Looking backward is one of our main hobbies here in the
American West, as we age. And we are aging, which could
mean we are growing up. Or not. It's a difficult process for
a culture that has always been so insistently boyish. Jack
Ray has been dead a long time now. As my father said, he
drank his liver right into the ground. "But, by God," my father said, "he was something once."

⌒

POSSIBILITY IS THE OLDEST American story. Head
west for freedom and the chance of inventing a spanking
new life for yourself. Our citizens are always leaping the
traces when their territory gets too small and cramped.

Back in the late '50s living with my wife and our small
children in our little cattle-ranch house, when things would
get too tight on a rainy Sunday afternoon in November I always had the excuse of work. "I got to go out," I would say,
and I would duck away to the peacefulness of driving the

muddy fields and levee banks in my old Ford pickup. Or, if
the roads were too bad, I would go down to the blacksmith
shop and bang on some damned thing.

*Whenever I find myself growing grim about the mouth;
whenever it is damp, drizzly November in my soul; whenever I find myself involuntarily pausing before coffin ware-
houses, and bringing up the rear of every funeral I meet. . . .*
Then he runs away to sea. *Ishmael.*

". . . lighting out for territory," says Huckleberry Finn,
with his brokenhearted optimism, right at the end of his
getaway down the Mississippi.

And it wasn't just the run-away boys in books. John
Colter left Ohio at the age of thirty, to head up the Missouri
with Lewis and Clark in 1804. He stayed west another five
years, earning his keep as a fur trapper in pursuit of the
beaver. One fearsome Montana winter he took a legendary
walk from Fort Lisa on the Yellowstone, traveling through
what is Yellowstone Park to circumnavigate the Tetons—
about a thousand miles on snowshoes through country
where no white man had ever been before. A thing both
wondrous and powerful drove him. Maybe it was a need so
simple as being out, away.

Imagine those shining snowy mountains burning against
the sheltering endless bowl of clean sky, and Colter alone
there in Jackson Hole. We will not see such things again, not
any of us, ever. It's gone. We know it is. Only one man ever
got to be Colter. Not even Bridger or Joe Meek or Jedediah
Smith had a world so absolutely to themselves. Except for
some natives, who maybe never thought they were alone.

In 1836 Narcissa and Marcus Whitman came west with
Eliza and Henry Spalding. The first white women had
crossed the Rockies. Along the way they witnessed one of
the last fur-trapper rendezvous, on the Green River in
Wyoming. Think of those Presbyterian women among the

inhabitants of wilderness. Less than ten years later Marcus Whitman was leading one of the first wagon trains west from St. Louis to Oregon country.

The New York newspaper editor Andrew Greely worried about the exodus, wondering what those families could be seeking, leaving behind the best of climates and agricultural lands, schools and churches and markets: "For what, then, do they brave the desert, the wilderness, the savage, the snowy precipices of the Rocky Mountains, the early summer march, the storm-drenched bivouac, and the gnawings of famine? Only to fulfill their destiny! There is probably not one among them whose outward circumstances will be improved by this perilous pilgrimage."

Anybody sensible, Greely suggested, would stop ". . . this side of the jumping-off place." The only practice stupider than such migration, he said, was suicide.

It's easy to understand his puzzlement. The wagon trains were predominantly middle-class ventures. Poor folks couldn't afford a wagon, much less provisions. The basic outfitting cost up toward a thousand dollars. And in those long-gone days that was some real money. But seemingly sensible people persisted in selling their good farms and heading west.

Imagine half the population of Ohio picking up sticks, selling out, and heading for one of our latter-day mythological frontiers, Alaska or Australia. Greely was right, it was crazy, it was a mania.

What was pushing them? Lots of things. Among them a quite legitimate fear of mortal corruption and death. Cholera. By the spring of 1849 an epidemic had reached St. Louis. Ten percent of the population died of the disease. The road west from Independence was likened to traveling through a graveyard.

But mostly, we have to believe, they were lured west by

promises. Promises of paradise for the taking. Free land, crystalline water, great herds of game roaming the natural meadowlands, good fishing, gold, all in unfettered abundance, a new world every morning.

What compelled men to believe promises of paradise on earth with such simpleminded devotion? Well, for openers, a gut yearning for the chance of becoming someone else, and freedom from the terrible weight of responsibilities, freedom too often equalling free, without cost.

My own great-grandfather on my father's side left Michigan in 1849 to travel down the Mississippi and across to Panama, where he hiked west through the jungles on the route Balboa had blazed and caught a ship north to California and the gold camps. After a long and bootless career of chasing mineral trace in the mountain streams, first in the central Sierra and then up around the foothills of Mount Shasta, he gave it up and turned to ranching and school teaching in one place after another around the Northwest, until in 1897 he died white-trash poor in the sagebrush backlands near Silver Lake, Oregon, leaving a family determined to shake his suicidal despair.

It wasn't just the gold that he never found—such instant boomer riches were to have been only the beginning. The green and easy dreamland fields of some home place were to have been the ultimate reward for his searching, the grape arbor beside the white house he would own outright, where he could rest out some last serene years while the hordes of grandchildren played down across the lawns by the sod-banked pond where the tame ducks swam and fed and squawked in their happy, idiot way. The pastoral heaven on this earth—some particular secret and heart's-desire version of it—has time and again proved to be the absolute heart in American dreams. All this we promise you.

CHILDHOOD, IT HAS BEEN SAID, is always partly a lie of poetry. When I was maybe eight years old, in the fall of the year, I would have to go out in the garden after school with damp burlap sacks and cover the long rows of cucumber and tomato plants, so they wouldn't freeze.

It was a hated, cold-handed job that had to be done every evening. I daydreamed along in a halfhearted, distracted way, flopping the sacks onto the plants, sorry for myself and angry because I was alone at my boring work. No doubt my younger brother and sister were in the house and warm. Eating cookies.

But then a great strutting bird appeared out from the dry remnants of our corn, black tail feathers flaring and a monstrous yellow-orange air-sack pulsating from its white breast, its throat croaking with popping sounds like rust in a joint.

The bird looked to be stalking me with grave slow intensity, coming after me from a place I could not understand as real, and yet quite recognizable, the sort of terrifying creature that would sometimes spawn in the incoherent world of my night-dreams. In my story, now, I say it looked like death, come to say hello. Then, it was simply an apparition.

The moment demanded all my boyish courage, but I stood my ground, holding one of those wet sacks out before me like a shield, stepping slowly backwards, listening as the terrible creature croaked, its bright preposterous throat pulsating—and then the great bird flapped its wings in an angry way, raising a little commonplace dust.

It was the dust, I think, that did it, convincing me that this could not be a dream. My fear collapsed, and I felt foolish as I understood this was a creature I had heard my father talk about, a courting sage-grouse, we called them prairie chickens. This was only a bird and not much interested in me at all. But for an instant it had been both phantom and real, the thing I deserved, come to punish me for my anger.

For that childhood moment I believed the world to be absolutely inhabited by an otherness that was utterly demonic and natural, not of my own making. But soon as that bird was enclosed in a story that defined it as a commonplace prairie chicken, I was no longer frightened. It is a skill we learn early, the art of inventing stories to explain away the fearful sacred strangeness of the world. Storytelling and make-believe, like war and agriculture, are among the arts of self-defense, and all of them are ways of enclosing otherness and claiming ownership.

Such emblematic memories continue to surface, as I grow older and find ways to accept them into the fiction of myself. One of the earliest, from a time before I ever went to school, is of studying the worn oiled softwood flooring in the Warner Valley store where my mother took me when she picked up the mail three times a week. I have no idea how many years that floor had been tromped and dirtied and swept, but by the time I recall it was worn into a topography of swales and buttes, traffic patterns and hard knots, much like the land, if you will, under the wear of a glacier. For a child, as his mother gossiped with the postmistress, it was a place, high ground and valleys, prospects and sanctuaries, and I in my boredom could invent stories about it—finding a coherency I loved, a place that was mine. They tore up that floor somewhere around the time I started school, and I had the sense to grieve.

The coherency I found worn into those floorboards was mirrored a few years later, just before the war began, when I was seven or eight, in the summertime play of my brother and sister and cousins and myself, as we laid out roads to drive and rectangular fields to work with our toy trucks in the dirt under the huge old box elder, which also functioned as a swing tree near the kitchen door to our house. It was a little play world we made for ourselves, and it was, we believed, just like the vast world beyond. In it we imitated the kind of ordering we watched each spring while our father laid out the garden with such measured precision, and the kind of planning we could not help but sense while riding with him along the levee banks in his dusty Chevrolet pickup truck. All the world we knew was visible from the front porch of our house, inside the valley, and all the work he did was directed toward making it orderly, functional, and productive—and of course that work seemed sacred.

Our play ended when a small rattlesnake showed up in our midst, undulating in sweeping little curving lines across our dusty make-believe fields. A young woman who cooked for my mother killed the snake in a matter-of-fact way with a shovel. But the next spring my mother insisted, and my father hauled in topsoil and planted the packed dirt, where we had played at our toylike world of fields, into a lawn where rattlesnakes would never come. We hated him for it.

These stories suggest reasons why, during childhood winters through the Second World War, such an important segment of my imagination lived amid maps of Europe and the Pacific. Maps delineated the dimensions of that dream which was the war for me, maps and traced drawings of aircraft camouflaged for combat. I collected them like peacetime city boys collect baseball cards, and I colored them in with crayons, my far South Pacific and Europe invaded and shaped by dreams and invisible forces I could not hope to make sense of any other way.

IN THE SPRING OF 1942, just before I turned ten years old, we opened every first-period class in our one-room Warner Valley schoolhouse singing *Praise the Lord and Pass the Ammunition.* We embraced the war. We heard it every morning on the Zenith Trans-Oceanic radio, while we got ready for school, and during recess we ran endless games of gunfighter pursuit and justifiably merciless death in the playgrounds. Mostly we killed Hitler and Mister Tojo.

Fall down, you're dead.

When it came your turn to play Nazi, you were honor bound to eventually fall killed through the long adult agony, twisting and staggering to heedless collapse in the dirt. Out in our landlocked, end-of-the-road, rancher valley, the air was bright and clean with purpose.

Always, at least in memory, those running battles involve my cousins and my younger brother and my even younger sister, and a black-and-white dog named Victory. Out back of the house in the summer of 1942 we circled and shot our ways through groves of wild plum in heavy fruit, and we swung to ambush from gnarled limbs in the apple orchard where the blue flies and the yellowjackets were mostly interested in having their way with the rotting fallen fruit: yellowjackets flitting to a hive in the hollow trunk of a Lombardy poplar along the irrigation ditch, burning the air with their going, and near to the secret, stinging, irreligious heart of *my* paradise.

IN LATE SEPTEMBER our dog named Victory was crushed under the rear duals of a semi-truck flatbed hauling 100-pound burlap sacks of my father's newly combined oats across 40 twisting miles of gravel road over the Warner Mountains to town and the railroad. My sister ran shrieking to the kitchen door, and my mother came to the roadside in her apron, and I was stoic and tough-minded as that poor animal panted and died. *Beyond the crystal sea, undreamed shores, precious angels.*

This was a time when our national life was gone to war against U-boats and Bataan and the death march, betrayal reeking everywhere. The death of that dog with cockleburrs matted into his coat must have shimmered with significance past heartbreak. We were American and proud, and we were steeled to deal with these matters.

So we unearthed a shallow grave in the good loam soil at the upper end of the huge rancher garden my father laid out each spring in those days, before it became cheaper to feed our crews from truckloads of canned goods bought wholesale in the cities. We gathered late-blooming flowers from the border beneath my mother's bedroom window, we loaded the stiffening carcass of that dead dog on a red wagon, and we staged a funeral with full symbolic honors.

My older cousin blew taps through his fist, my brother hid his face, and my six-year-old sister wept openly, which was all right since she was a little child. I waved a leafy bough of willow over the slope-sided grave while my other cousins shoveled the loose dry soil down on the corpse.

It is impossible to know what the child who was myself felt, gazing east across the valley that I can still envision so clearly—the ordered garden and the sage-covered slope running down to the slough-cut meadows of the Thompson Field, willows there concealing secret hideaway places where I would burrow away from the world for hours, imagining I was some animal, hidden and watching the stock cows graze the open islands of meadow grass.

On the far side of the valley lay the great level distances of the plow-ground fields that had so recently been tule swamps, reaching to the rise of barren eastern ridges. That enclosed valley is the home I imagine walking when someday I fall into the dream that is my death. My real, particular, vivid and populated solace for that irrevocable moment of utter loss when the mind stops forever. The chill of that

remembered September evening feels right as I imagine
that heartbreakingly distant boy.

~~

IT'S HARD FOR ME to know where I got the notion of
waving that willow branch over our burial of that poor dog
unless I find it in this other memory, from about the same
time. A Paiute girl of roughly my own age died of measles in
the ramshackle encampment her people maintained alongside the irrigation ditch that eventually led to our vast
garden. A dozen or so people lived there, and true or not, I
keep thinking of them as in touch with some remnant memories of hunting and gathering forebears who summered so
many generations in the valley we had so recently come to
own.

In the fall of 1890 a man named James Mooney went
west under the auspices of the Bureau of Ethnology to in-
vestigate the rise of Native American religious fervor that
culminated in the massacre at Wounded Knee on Decem-
ber 29. In Mooney's report, *The Ghost Dance Religion and
the Sioux Outbreak of 1890,* there is a statement delivered
by a Paiute man named Captain Dick at Fort Bidwell in
Surprise Valley—right in the home territory I am talking
about, at the junction on maps where California and Nevada
come together at the Oregon border.

> All Indians must dance, everywhere, keep on danc-
> ing. Pretty soon in the next spring Big Man come.
> He bring back game of every kind. The game be
> thick everywhere. All dead Indians come back and
> live again. They all be strong just like young men,
> be young again. Old blind Indians see again and get
> young and have fine time. When the Old Man comes
> this way, then all the Indians go to the mountains,

high up away from the whites. Whites can't hurt the
Indians then. Then while Indians way up high, big
flood comes like water and all white people die, get
drowned. After that water go away and then nobody but Indians everywhere game all kinds thick.
Then medicine-man tell Indians to send word to all
Indians to keep up dancing and the good time will
come. Indians who don't dance, who don't believe
in this word, will grow little, just about a foot high,
and stay that way. Some of them will turn into wood
and will be burned in the fire.

In the 1950s and '60s a Paiute named Conlan Dick
lived in a cabin on our ranch in Warner Valley and helped
to look after the irrigation and fences. Conlan was reputed
to be a kind of medicine-man in our local mythology, related
to the man who delivered that statement. His wife, whose
name I cannot recall, did ironing for women in the valley.
And there was a son, a young man named Virgil Dick, who
sometimes came to Warner for a few weeks and helped his
father with the field work.

In the early 1960s my cousin, the one who blew taps
through his fist in 1942, was riding horseback across the
swampy spring meadows alongside Conlan. He asked if
Virgil was Conlan's only child.

Conlan grinned. "Naw," he said. "But you know, those
kids, they play outside, and they get sick and they die."

Story after story. Is it possible to claim that proceeding
through some incidents in this free-associative manner is in
fact a technique, a way of discovery? Probably. One of our
model narrators these days is the patient spinning and
respinning the past and trying to resolve it into a story that
makes sense.

"... they get sick and they die." Once I had the romance

in me to think that this was the mature comment of a man who had grown up healed into wholeness and connection with the ways of nature to a degree I would never understand. Now I think it was more likely the statement of a man trying to forget his wounds—so many of which were inflicted by school-yard warriors like us. A healthy culture could never have taught him to forego sorrow.

In any event, Captain Dick's magic was dead.

All these stories are part of my own story about a place called Home, and a time in which I imagined we owned it all. The girl who died was named Pearl. I recall her name with that particular exactness which occasionally hovers in memories. She was of enormous interest to us because she so obviously disdained our foolish play with make-believe weapons and miniature trucks. Or so it seemed. Maybe she was only shy or had been warned away from us. But to our minds she lived with adults and shared in the realities of adult lives in ways we did not, and now she was being paid the attention of burial.

Try to imagine their singing that spring morning. I cannot. I like to think our running brigade of warrior children might have been touched by dim sorrow-filled wailing in the crystalline brightness of her morning, but the memory is silent.

Maybe its enough to recall the sight of people she loved, carrying her elaborately clothed body in an open home-built casket. Not that we saw it up close, or that we ever really saw a body, clothed or unclothed.

They were making their slow parade up a sandy path through the sagebrush to her burial in the brushy plot, loosely fenced with barbed wire, which we knew as the "Indian Graveyard." I see them high on the banking sand-hill behind our house, and beyond them the abrupt 2,000-foot lift of rimrock that forms the great western lip of our

Warner Valley. That rim is always there, the table of lava-flow at the top breaking so abruptly, dropping through long scree-slopes clustered with juniper. As I grow older it is always at my back. The sun sets there, summer and winter. I can turn and squint my eyes and see it.

From the flowering trees in the homesteader's orchard behind our house we watched that astonishing processional through my father's binoculars, and then we ran out through the brush beyond the garden, tasting the perfect spring morning and leaping along the small animal trails, filled with thrilling purpose, and silent and urgent. We had to be closer.

The procession was just above us on the sandy trail when we halted, those people paying us no mind but frightening us anyway, mourning men and women in their dark castaway clothing and bright blankets and strange robes made of animal skins, clutching at spring blossoms and sweeping at the air with thick sheaves of willow in new leaf. It is now that I would like to hear the faint singsong of their chanting. I would like to think we studied them through the dancing waves of oncoming heat, and found in them the only models we had ever had for such primal ceremonies.

But this keeps becoming fiction. Ours was a rising class of agricultural people, new to that part of the world, too preoccupied with an endless ambition toward perfection in their work to care at all for any tradition of religion. No one in our immediate families had ever died, and no one ever would so far as we knew. None of us, in those days, had any interest in religion or ritual.

So I have this story of those shrouded people proceeding through my imagination. I feel them celebrating as that young girl entered into the ripe fruit of another paradise, lamenting the dole-food exigencies of their own lives, some of them likely thinking she was lucky to have escaped.

But I don't really have much idea what was going on behind the story I've made of that morning. It was is if those people were trailing along that sandy path toward tomorrow land themselves. Some of them, somewhere, are likely still alive.

In a book called *Shoshone,* the poet Ed Dorn tells of interviewing an ancient man and woman in a trailer house on the Duck Valley Reservation, a couple of hundred miles east of us but still deep in the high basin and range desert, along the border between Idaho and Nevada. They were both more than one hundred years old and told Dorn they had never heard of white men until past the age of thirty. Which is possible.

It's easy to imagine those ancient people grinning in what looks to be a toothless old way in their aluminum-sided trailer house, with screens on the windows, on the Duck Valley Reservation. They must have understood the value of stories. Dorn says they demanded cartons of cigarettes before they allowed themselves to be photographed. The point is, they were willing to be part of any make-believe anybody could invent for them, willing to tell their stories and let us make of them what we could. But not for nothing. Stories are valuable precisely to the degree that they are for the moment useful in our ongoing task of finding coherency in the world, and those old people must have known that whatever story Dorn was imagining was worth at least the price of some smokes.

My father's catskinners bulldozed the shacktown Indian camp with its willow-roofed ramada into a pile of old posts and lumber and burned it, after the last of those people had gone to wherever they went. Our children? In the fall of 1942, the same year that girl named Pearl was buried, they learned something about the emotional thrust of a warrior code as the news from Zenith Trans-Oceanic radio was translated into singing in first-period music class, and they loaded that dead dog named Victory in a red wagon and trailed him toward burial at the upper end of the garden. And I waved sweeps of willow over the ceremony while my cousin blew taps through his fist.

Buckaroos

ONE SURE THING about us boys on those old dust-eating summery afternoons during World War II, out there branding MC calves on the high deserts, we dreamed of highways and rodeo. But that country of northern Nevada and southeastern Oregon is like an ancient hidden kingdom. Change and escape do not come easy there.

Owyhee. Sounds like Hawaii. In 1819 Donald MacKenzie brought one of the first brigades of fur trappers into the Snake River country, coming from the mouth of the Columbia, and he brought with him a few Hawaiians. He sent them off to explore the uncharted river that came into the Snake from the south, through the desert barrens. The Hawaiians never came back. The river and territory inherited their name.

This is a story of going back, on the road and seeking romance and Hawaiians in the desert, crystal fountains of my own making, and mountain-man hubris. What I wanted was Nevada, and *laissez faire,* hard-way sixes at four o'clock in the morning and then, if it should suit my fancy, a quiet drink on the terrace with myself and the sunrise, like a grown-up in the land where everybody gets to do what they want to do.

Specifically, I was heading to visit the chuckwagon buckaroo outfit run by the IL Ranch, on the edge of the Owyhee desert north of Tuscarora, Nevada. The IL is an outfit run in the old and sensible way, four horses pulling the wagon, and no trucks and no town cars and no horse trailers. Just the men and the livestock and the countryside, settling into a routine with one another amid the turns of season.

The fist branding of the spring season was to be the next morning, if the weather cleared. The smell of branding was one of the wistful things I had come looking for. But the storms had been driving in from the west, spitting snow and rain, and the prospects did not look good. The hot branding iron scalds and blots on the hides of wet calves.

FEARFUL THAT THE DESERT would be all muddy roads and bad news, I skipped the Tuscarora turnoff and went on into Elko, one of those two-hearted Nevada ranching and gambling towns that grew up at the end of the nineteenth century after the Union Pacific traced the route of California-bound wagon trains along the Humboldt River. Up on the hill, in the shade of box elder, you have country people mowing their lawns and reading the *Western Horseman* magazine on their patios, while down by the interstate you've got gambling everywhere and bars that never close, and always, off on the exotic edges of what I knew from high school, the dangerous reek of prostitution.

Those whorehouses put me in a you-can't-go-home-again quandary of the most elemental kind. Back deep in the misty past there is this land inhabited by dreams and passions, and you love it—your daddy was rich and your momma good looking—and you want it to be all perfection, bronzed in your memory like baby shoes. And whorehouses, well, I just don't know.

There was a time I liked them fine. In Klamath Falls, Oregon, where we wintered when I was in high school, there were five houses, places with names like the *Iron Door* and the *Palm Hotel.* There was a whole crowd of us growing boys who ruined our athletic careers by hanging out in those homes for the misbegotten eros of the times. We were there a lot. And why not? Say it's Friday night in February and the basketball game is over, and the alternative is the sock-hop mixer down at the Teen Age Club. Lots of leaning against the wall and studying your look-alike basketball rivals from out of town while the girls dance with one another. Pretty soon somebody says, "Let's go," and you nod in your cool-eyed way and all drift down to the Iron Door.

And there were summers, over in Lakeview, Oregon, near the ranch where I grew up. Riding with the wagon on the desert, or working in the hay fields, I was earning a man's wages by the time I was fifteen or so, and summers were a different ballgame. Out beyond the rodeo grounds there was a whorehouse district called Hollywood. And it was official—the houses paid taxes into a special city fund for streetlights. This was all part of the timeless rationale you would hear, the basic argument to do with ensuring the safety of decent women: sex-crazed ranch hands could work out their primitive lusts down in Hollywood and not wander the streets, molesting wives and mothers. And besides, how about those streetlights? Hollywood, I guess, was a kind of civic sacrifice area.

The girls, some not much older than we were, would serve us boys with whiskey and take our money and smile and laugh with us so long as we could pay our way. Those houses sided with tar paper were not places to contemplate romance or running away with your darling, but they were where so many of us received our most formidable training for manhood, learning the most central message of western civilization: do not break you heart over anything resembling promiscuity; property remains. It was the same message my grandfather had been teaching me all my life.

Sitting there in my Elko motel room, sipping at a wonderful little square pint bottle of Jack Daniel's whiskey, I could not bring myself to drift back down to the cathouses. Like Hemingway said in another context, and he is our patron in these matters, ". . . the war was always there, but we did not go to it any more."

All of it, there in Elko, was like coming home. In the J. M. Capriola Company on Commercial Street I wandered around just touching the gear, rawhide riatas and horsehair mecates, rubbing my hands over the $1,500 working buckaroo saddles, eyeing the silver-mounted Garcia spurs and Spanish bits and belt buckles in their glass cases, feeling a pang of awe at the way prices had gone up.

At Capriola's, a complete gear-up for a desert horseback working man—saddle, bridle, Spanish and snaffle bits, chinks (the chaps they wear in the buckaroo north country, cut off at the knee), tepee camp tent, hobbles plus a pair of woolly sheepskin chaps for winter, bedroll and blankets— will run well beyond $3,000. Which is a load of money for a working cowhand, even if he gets board and room free. But the gear is built to accompany a working person through a good many seasons of serious endeavor, all up and down the road.

And downstairs in the Commercial Hotel were the crap tables and the mounted upright figure of what is reputed to be the largest white polar bear ever killed, taken by native hunters off Point Hope, Alaska. At midnight the Commercial was Point Hope for everybody; the last stand of your most basic American fantasy, if you could cloud your mind and write off a $276 run of bad karma in the midst of those hard-way sixes. Which was an art I was practicing, along about midnight in Elko, the land of the free.

So when morning dawned bright, rain clouds gone, I was ready for my trip out past Tuscarora to the IL. For me it was like going back in time.

The headquarters of the IL Ranch is on the Owyhee South Fork, edged up on the sage hills above about 2,500 acres of native meadow hay land. Off west is the enormous rimrock flatland of the Owyhee desert, elevation always over 5,000 feet, reaching to the far-away Santa Rosa mountains, 70 miles by air, over 9,000 feet and still snow-covered in mid-May. About 20 miles east there's Jack's Peak, rising 10,000 feet in the Independence Mountains over the Columbia Basin, where the IL cattle and sheep run during the late summer and early fall.

If Elko smelled like home, this *was* home. Down in a cramped little office next to the cookhouse I met the ranch boss, Bill Maupin, and his wife, Wanda, and the sheep boss, Allen King, who was up from the sheep range, which is on the south side of the Humboldt River, far to the west between Battle Mountain and Winnemucca.

The IL ranch runs about 5,000 mother cows and another 5,000 head of sheep on about 480,000 acres of deeded and government-leased land. And it is the smallest of the major spreads in that country. The Petan Ranch to the north, the Spanish Ranch, which headquarters over in the Independence Valley northeast of Tuscarora, and the Garvey Ranch to the west in Paradise Valley—they're all bigger, at least by reputation.

It's regarded as rude to ask a man how much property he owns. But there is one good story about a man named John G. Taylor, who was an early owner of the IL. Seems he was tired of hearing about the Miller and Lux Ranch. Around the beginning of this century it was claimed a man could ride from Burns in Oregon to the south end of the San Joaquin Valley in California and camp every night but one on Miller and Lux land. That's the version I always heard.

"Damn, I don't know about that," John G. Taylor is supposed to have said, "but I do know this. I can walk on the backs of my own sheep from Lovelock to the three forks of the Owyhee River." That would be maybe 150 miles.

A BUCKAROO AT THE IL RANCH, if he's been around long enough to build himself a reputation, might draw as much as $500 a month, board and all the room he wants for his bedroll. Those are standard wages in the country. Hard work, and you've got to respect it if you want the job. But it's a life to which a lot of people, in a complex variety of ways, are returning. Turning back to livestock and the long wheel of days, and some chance at self-knowledge, or at least some knowledge of who killed the cow you are eating.

On the way to where the IL wagon crew was branding, about twenty miles west from headquarters, Bill Maupin pointed out the ruins of an old stone house sitting grand and alone alongside a mostly wet-weather creek. The story is that a Mormon man built it around 1900 and brought his three wives to live there. Two of the wives died that winter and he buried them in the basement, since all the ground outside was frozen hard as metal. The joke was that those women winterkilled.

She is a wonderful country, go the intimations, but a good place to be careful every chance you get. If you are going alone—into your radical mountain-man independence and isolation and loneliness—think ahead and take precautions.

Winterkilled. Brings to mind another charming old saying: "She is hard country on women and horses." Which means, I guess, that men and mules can make out all right and have a swell time digging graves in the basement.

This country fosters a kind of woman who never seems to bother about who she is supposed to be, mainly because there is always work, and getting it done in a level-eyed way is what counts most. Getting the work done, on horseback or not, and dicing their troubles into jokes. These women wind up looking 50 when they are 37 and 53 when they are 70. It's as though they wear down to what counts and just last there, fine and staring the devil in the eye every morning.

Bill Maupin pointed out a place where a dead man had been found with three silver dollars in his pocket, near the edge of a sandy wash through the sagebrush. One morning, years ago, the buckaroo crew from the IL had come across the fellow, dead of natural causes from what anybody could tell, sitting in a buggy, white eyes open to the new sun. The sheriff came out from Elko, looked him over and blessed him, and they buried him where they found him, the three shining silver dollars in his pocket for luck.

The country is thick with such stories. Unknown travelers. Bill Maupin was not so much telling me things about people whose lives he cherished as he was wondering if I shared his reverence for those old work-centered men and women who showed us how to live on that desert.

And, yeah, I did. Bill Maupin and I grew up knowing a lot of the same people, and surely the same kind of people. The cow boss at the IL, Tom Anderson, turned out to be a man I had just missed knowing when we were both younger. Tom broke in buckarooing on the MC just after I went away to the Air Force. Hugh Cahill and old man Ross Dollarhide were running the MC wagon then.

IN THIS MEMORY, our kid is maybe eleven years old and catching horses every morning before sunrise out on our high desert country of southeastern Oregon. The remuda would circle in one of those old stone corrals, and the alkaline dust would lift in a clear string to the blooming bowl of sky. I was learning responsibility in a ranching country of great distances and silences, where the history is a story of ranching people and their dreams.

My grandfather, during the hard times of the Great Depression, had yielded to one of those dreams and staked the property he spent a lifetime accumulating in order to get his hands on one of the great ranches, the MC in Warner Valley, out east of Lakeview and part of the local mythology: some twenty-odd thousand acres of peat-soil swamplands in the valley, and what seemed in those horseback days to be endless summer range out east on the desert. A million or so acres, that desert range was mostly Taylor grazing land leased from the Federal government, but my grandfather treated it like it was his own.

Before the end of World War II there was no asphalt within thirty-five miles of headquarters on the MC. No telephones; a Delco generator for electricity. A great deal of time was spent in the company of animals, talking to yourself.

Which was fine. You would slow down and get used to the pace. *Going to the desert*—that's what we called summering out there with the cattle—ten or so riders, a chuckwagon and cook and no automobiles until somewhere in the middle of the war. Clevon Dixon, who was cow boss on the MC in the 1960s, said the quiet just took you over.

"First week," he'd say, "I always hate it, wondering what's happening somewhere. Second week I don't care so much. After that I can't imagine anyplace else, and I don't ever want to turn back toward town. If it wasn't for winter, you could stay out there forever."

THAT COUNTRY I CAME FROM in southeastern Oregon and northern Nevada is a land of great ranches: the IL and the Whitehorse, the MC and the ZX and Peter French's great P Ranch, which has been owned by the Federal government since the 1930s, miles of swampland meadow along the Donner und Blitzen River, a wildlife refuge these days. History there is a story of ranches and dreams of empire, of land and cattle and great horsemen, but it is more a history of getting the work done, feeding cattle from a creaking hay wagon while the snow blows level to the ground in late January.

My education in such realities began with men like Ross Dollarhide, who lived to see ninety years, and died in bed, having endured. The way legends should end.

The MC was like a feudal kingdom in those days, not many neighbors you ever saw, nobody around for the most part but our family and the people who worked for them, a world centered on horses and cattle those years before the end of World War II, when everybody went to pickup trucks and tractors. When we lost the family farm in Montana, an old man told me, was when we went to the goddamned tractors. Maybe so.

Anyway, there I was, eleven years old, learning the business. It was late June, and we were branding calves alongside a little alkaline sink on the Gooch Plateau, right near the Oregon/Nevada border. Ross Dollarhide was wagon boss for the MC buckaroo outfit at the time, in charge of the riders, a cook, chuckwagon and 65 or 70 head of horses in the remuda, looking after the more than 6,000 Hereford cows and their calves, which my grandfather was summering in the desert. And maybe 500 head of bulls, purebreds, from places like Wyoming and Montana, shipped in on the railroad so there was no chance of inbreeding.

Dollarhide was as old as my grandfather, and he was my main example of how to live like a man in the world. Ross had been a legend in the country since he rode into the Whitehorse Ranch on a fat-tired bicycle the summer he was sixteen around 1900, and announced he was looking for work, riding rough horses if there was a choice. Which is the way legends get started.

According to this one, the old hands grinned, and put him up on some Roman-nosed gray stud nobody had even thought about trying to ride. We know the rest, that devil horse bucked down to a stalled and sweaty, bloody-mouthed froth—even rode to death in some versions of the fireside tale—and young Dollarhide triumphant, the old-timers shaking their heads and smiling.

"We got one," they would say. "A real one." He was a real one to us, for sure, and we all believed some version of that story. Dollarhide was a great horseman, and he had earned and deserved any esteem the world might grant. We rode out each morning behind a legendary man, and we knew it. At least I did, when I was eleven.

So I was amazed to see him pulling leather like any greenhorn on that day in late June when we were branding calves out there on the Gooch Plateau. We had gathered maybe a hundred range cows and their spring calves out of the low hills off south, driven them down across a lava-rock flat, built a fire of greasewood and sage to heat the MC irons, and we were just getting started. A couple of the old roper hands, Dollarhide among them, would ride into the herd and hindfoot the calves with their tight-woven rawhide riatas and drag them to the fire where three or four of the strong young bucks were doing the ground work, the acrid smoke of burning hair and hide lofting around them and their hands bloody as they notched the ears and castrated the little bull calves with their thin-bladed knives. It was hard scab-handed work, and dangerous if you were new to it, or just awkward and given to daydreaming.

I was all those things, so I was among the three or four who were left with the tiresome job we called "holding cows." We were stationed around the perimeter of the little herd, just keeping the cows and their calves together in a milling way until the ropers had done their work, and Dollarhide shouted, and another branding was finished. What we mostly did was sit quietly beyond the fringes of

the herd on whatever horse it was that day, and wait to ride
on and gather and brand another 70 or 100 calves before
heading back in the late afternoon to the wagon, camped at
Rock Spring or South Corral or one of those places, traveling at the long, jolting, killer pace Dollarhide preferred, all
of us strung out behind, across the sage flats and going to
our second and last meal of the day, hoping maybe the cook
had opened a few cans of chilled tomatoes to go with the
fried steak and milk gravy and chopped spuds and biscuits.
Canned tomatoes were our main fruit dish on that desert,
where a drink of spring water was a luxury and pancake
syrup mixed with butter was our candy.

Maybe I was dreaming of some such thing when Dollarhide, right before me, got himself in quick and unimagin-
able trouble. He was riding a long-legged traveling horse, a
black with three white stockings and not much in the way
of brains, a big four-year-old one of the young bucks had
broken to the bridle that spring. The horse was just learning the rudiments of calf roping. There had been a lot of
brainless skittering and crow-hopping around, but nothing
serious while the old man roped and dragged a couple of
small calves. But then he swung a big loop and caught himself a yearling bull calf that had been missed by this same
branding crew the previous fall, caught that bull calf right
around the middle, and the rodeo got started.

The yearling weighted close to 500 pounds, all quick
bullish energy, and he ducked himself sideways and backwards just as Dollarhide dropped the loop at him—one
of those things that happen every so often in a chancy
world—and there you had the situation: that yearling bull
calf caught secure around the belly and not by the hind feet
at all, surprising the old man, who had maybe been paying
more attention to this knot-headed horse than to his roping;

the yearling cutting back in a wide swing, and Dollarhide already cursing as he spurred that long-legged horse, trying to get its head around to face the rope.

The rest of it was slow motion. The rawhide riata came cutting up under the black horse's tail, and the horse goosed it clear loose, just going straight up and coming down into a twisting bucking exhibition that would have looked fine in Champion of the World competitions. Dollarhide had seen what was coming and already had turned loose his turns of rope on the saddle horn, getting clear rid of the riata, but he was halfways unseated by surprise, and they were out in the rocks and brush, the stocking-footed gelding plunging and nearly falling and then going high in another twisting leap. Looked like the old man was in danger of coming down hard, and this was no joke, not for anybody, out in those lava rocks. A young man might escape with bad bruises and cuts, but a man of sixty might likely break in two or three places.

Then I saw it: the old man got hold of the saddle horn with both hands, and he pulled leather, and he stayed up there, out of his stirrups and everywhere on that gone-crazy horse, but up there and not down. He made the ride, nothing clean and pretty and competition about it, his head snapping and hat gone, those lava boulders with their etchings of lichen all around him if he should come loose, our legendary rider pulling leather like a child until the gelding wore down, and then Dollarhide was back in the saddle secure, the show was over.

The old man spurred the gelding, and came trotting back to us, the both of them breathless. A little whirlwind of craziness had gone by, leaving nothing much damaged but my belief in legends. Dollarhide got down off the gelding, rolled a cigarette, put his hat back on his head, and caught me staring, read my mind. "Boy," he said, "this ain't a time to get killed. Not for wages."

RODEO MEMORIES. When I was a boy on the desert we dreamed of rodeos and those tight-bodied little buckle-chasing bunnies who used to hang around behind the bucking chutes, high-crowned white straw hats tipped back and wide purple ribbons trailing down to their asses. You know, the horn blows, the ride has been nothing but a rocking chair, and you kick loose and land running and then limp your way back to the chutes while the crowd goes on cheering. And there she is. Perfect teeth. Dreaming her own dreams.

We had a lot of those fantasies, late evenings around the cook fire after a back-breaking day in the scab-rock country between South Corral and Sage Hen Springs, where I served my horseback apprenticeship. "They're gonna put me in the movies, they're gonna make a big star out of me."

Or not. Maybe we always suspected, as part of our suspicion of anything eastern and citified, that any dream of rodeo always had at its center a sinkhole spiraling down toward night-town, drunk-man darkness and brain damage or moral failures of the most devastating kind. Or lost and pointless death, the kind that always happens to somebody else, like asphyxiation in the backseat of a secondhand car while it idles in a wintertime drive-in movie south of Bakersfield, California.

That happened to somebody I knew.

Even glory had its dark-side-of-the moon aspects. Back at the IL chuck tent, sipping coffee and eating fresh-baked apple pie, Tom Anderson and I talked about old man Dollarhide and his son, young Ross, who is dead, too, and the night young Ross fought Beef Miller outside Hunters Lodge in Lakeview, and Tootie Gunderson, who was tending bar that long-ago night—wondering what had become of her. Last either of us knew she was running a bar down in Cottonwood, California.

That fight with Beef Miller had to do with Ross having been Champion of the World at bulldogging sometime around 1953, with the huge silver buckle on his belt, and with him being white and Beef being Indian and the essential crookedness—racist and otherwise—of rodeo judging, and all the other resentments inherent therein. It wasn't any joke, and it isn't one in hindsight. Two large men, and they beat each other bloody. The next day I was sick drunk in the hay field.

I only saw Ross Dollarhide one more time, ten years later in the summer of 1963. Imagine way off to the west there is a technicolor glow to the sunset scheme of things over Warner Valley, vivid pink shadows coming down into our valley and in the sky a crossing of feathery disintegrating jet-stream contrails. I had watched my first Beatles concert on our only channel of television, and I sensed that uncanny things were beginning out there in the Great World. I was not taking part. I was home in the deep West, and because of that my life was lost.

This particular evening I was irrigating, which is a different process than may immediately come to mind, that art we called "balancing water," adjusting headgates and running pumps along our hundred or so miles of interwoven canal system, making sure nothing flooded before morning. None of that mucking around with a #2 shovel, no hip boots; but ramming along levee banks in a 1961 Ford pickup at fifty miles an hour, turning things on and off. Balancing water, and attempting to balance my perfect country life against desire. Barely coming up in long even rows against the sunset light and timothy in the meadows, waterbirds going north to their summer life on the tundra, my children and their horse, my wife in our home, and so much more, all against the burning of sour envy. I wanted to be somewhere else, nearby to that mysterious frenzy of energy echoing around those dim, grainy pictures of the Beatles and their manic hordes. I wanted to be riding and drifting into their high times.

And along comes trouble. Across the middle of our valley, a couple of years before, the state had built a highway that connected us to Winnemucca down in Nevada and ran on to the west. "Winnemucca to the Sea," it was called, as if honoring some need to always think westward. After I parked and opened the wire gate into the Big Beef Field, I heard the soft humming of an oncoming automobile traveling toward me with all the speed built up on that long 100-mile-an-hour voyage across the deserts of northern Nevada. With the gate open, I stood and watched it come at me out of the twilight.

It was a pink Cadillac convertible of that tailfin era, running without headlights. It began to slow and ended up coasting to a halt on the highway alongside where I stood. The top was down and the dark bareheaded man riding shotgun was someone I knew, but I hadn't seen in years, Ross Dollarhide the Younger, a man who by that time was living his life mostly in Los Angeles, on the fringes of the movie business, near the heart of mythology. The driver was another rodeo cowboy whose name I forget, a compact little blond fellow who never seemed to say anything but "Damn straight." Otherwise, the cat had got his tongue.

But Ross was another matter. A huge and agile man, by that time he had broken one of his legs so many times, and ridden with it broken, that he was forced to wear a steel brace strapped on the outside in his Levis. That brace was like an emblem of courage and heedlessness.

Ross handed me a warm quart of Miller's and climbed out to stand beside me in the twilight. He wanted to talk. Ross was maybe five years older than I, and an authentic rodeo hero. When I was a kid working summers around the desert chuckwagon, Ross was riding the rough string. So we knew each other, in the way little kids know the schoolyard big kids, and vice versa. And now here I was, working like a farmer for wages, and there he was, a former Champion of the World sporting that emblematic steel brace and wearing his silver-and-gold Champion of the World buckle, traveling in a pink Cadillac with no front windshield. The windshield was not broken out, but missing entirely, as if it had never been there.

"Looks like a windy sonofabitch," I said.

"Damn straight," said the driver, studying the road ahead.

Ross paid us no attention.

"If this is not pretty," he said, "would you take a look at this?" Ross leaned close and the odor of lemon shaving lotion was fairly overwhelming.

"What's that?" I said.

"Bugs. I got bugs plastered all over my face."

Thinking back about Ross and the bugs, I am reminded of Gregory Peck in *The Gunfighter,* sitting under a clock in the glow of his barroom gunfighter fame, waiting as destiny gallops closer, knowing well that in the real West it was horsemanship, not skill with a six-gun, that defined a man. Knowing he had gone wrong.

"Thirty-four years old," Gregory Peck said, "and I never even owned a decent watch." He was seriously saddened by the fact, as Ross was by the mosquitoes.

The conversation never got beyond that, but I knew what Ross was telling me. Foolishness. He felt trapped by a foolish sport he had mistaken for a purpose. As I felt trapped in agriculture. They drove away and I went on about balancing my water, the warm quart of Miller's between my knees as I drove, dumb with yearning to be along for the ride on that wandering adventure, if that's what it was.

From the vantage of these years later I see that both Ross and I were mourning the demise of an older sense of what was proper, in which I would not have envied his venturesome skills, and he would not have looked at my foot-soldier life as anything he needed.

We were grieving for the world of his father and my grandfather. Although the elder Dollarhide, the old man, never owned an acre of ground anywhere I knew about, and my grandfather made a concerted effort to own them all, they were equal men before the world in a real and quite unromantic way. Property, in that old world, did not make the man, but rather something about being centered in life, in what was happening right at the moment. To understand, all you had to do was watch old man Dollarhide cutting dry cows from the cows and calves in the fall of the year on a quick little bay horse named Tinkertoy, the old man never suspecting the importance of anything beyond what he was doing, or at least never letting on. It was loss of such undivided minds and lives, nostalgia for work that mattered and a rangeland sense of proportion—those were getting at us both; loss of a direct knowledge of what to do next and who we were supposed to be.

Now I grieve for Ross Dollarhide the Younger. He died in Flagstaff, Arizona, killed while working as a movie extra. His horse fell, and Ross took a rib through a lung. Apparently Ross just roughed it out in that old cowboy way, and didn't say anything about needing a medical man, and went back to his motel room and drowned in his blood some time in the night, trying to sleep. The story goes like that. Confusion and things carried too far, and another ultimate loss.

WHEN I WAS A KID we used to talk about those great silver and gold buckles, your name engraved under those magic words that will turn all the rest of your life just the slightest degree anticlimactic: *Champion of the World.* We used to guess at how much they would weigh, what they would feel like on your belt.

An existence thick with dreams. The young boys branding there that morning on the IL Ranch were like ghosts of what I most seriously wanted for a long time in my life. While they were roping and dragging calves, I cooked myself a half-dozen nuts—mountain oysters, testicles, whatever you know them by—on that juniper fire, right there nestling on the glowing charcoal. As I chewed them I got myself centered back into what I had once been. I found myself understanding what I had gone away hunting and why coming back here was not a sappy sentiment-filled thing to do.

In the summer of 1945 I was thirteen and we were haying the IXL, a little ranch my grandfather leased from the Charles Sheldon Antelope Refuge in Nevada, just south of the Oregon border in Guano Valley. Every summer the buckaroos had to hay that place. Took us maybe three weeks and kept us busy during the slack season. At least nobody had gone to tractors yet.

There were ten or twelve of us, counting the kids, me and my cousin and the wrango boy. As much as anything, this story is about the wrango boy, the kid who herded the horses and hauled firewood and water for the cook, sometimes doing a stint at peeling potatoes. Because that wrango boy, more than any of us, I think, had his eye on the Great World, those possibilities. All the past month we had been riding bucking horses after supper and most of the day on Sundays. Somebody had their bucking string running in the hills back of the IXL. We built a bucking chute in a stout round corral and the fun was on.

God, did I hate it. One thing I would never claim is any ability on horseback. Every Sunday I would get pitched into the fence or onto my head about three times. But this wrango boy was different. He rode those bucking horses as if they were a natural easy chair, and I've got no doubt that rodeo looked to him like a getaway route. From what, I don't know. Probably things to do with family and poverty.

But right then, in August of 1945, for that crew of men isolated way out there on the great highland desert, VJ Day must have looked like another kind of escape. Maybe just from the daily passage of commonplace life. An excuse for fun. Maybe from guilt at having taken an agricultural deferment from the Army, and avoided the fighting. Those were grave matters.

Anyway, all of them, nine or ten men in old man Dollarhide's black V-8 Ford, headed off on the eighty-five dusty miles to Denio and the nearest barroom. They came back the next morning with cases of whiskey and beer, and soon we were all drunk, even the chuckwagon cook, an old man named Jack Frost. It was my first time, and I stayed drunk for two days.

About noon it was decided we should move camp to the Doherty Place, an old starved-out homesteader ranch up in the middle of Guano Valley, just off from where the Winnemucca highway passes now. The men took the wagon, and we kids moved the horse herd at a long hard run for around twelve miles. For some reason there were no tragedies. I remember playing hand grenade with canned corn and dropping sacks of flour from the second-story windows at the Doherty Place like high-level bombers, watching them burst on the backs of horses. And finally we threw all the food into the open well and the men left again in the Ford.

The next morning we were alone, we three kids and the old cook. He was howling drunk in his bed, stinking of urine, and could not get up. We were still somewhat drunked up, but we managed to harness the teams and load the wagon, including old soggy Jack, who was still in his bed and muttering about dying, and headed for the MC Ranch headquarters, fifty miles across the rutted desert roads to Warner Valley.

My cousin and I puled chickenshit rank. Because our grandfather owned them, we took the horses and left the wrango boy with the wagon. By midafternoon we were turning 100 saddle horses loose on the meadows near the ranch house. The wrango boy was two days getting there with the chuckwagon and that poor old cook in his bed, all the time lamenting and threatening to die. A little later, in Lakeview for the Labor Day rodeo, the last time I ever saw him, that boy looked at me with hot eyes and said, "That is it for you sons-a-bitches."

We were in one of those old double-duty barber shops, which are gone from the country now, where a man in off the desert could get himself shaved and have his hair cut and then take himself an opulent two-hour bath, all the hot water you wanted for $1.50. And then get into fresh clothes from the skin out and be ready for town. That fellow, the former wrango boy, stood there looking at me slick-faced, his hair combed down and wet, wearing a new yellow shirt bought around the corner at the Lakeview Mercantile, and all at once he was a grown-up and I wasn't. He just shook his head and turned away.

What he was telling me was simple. At maybe fifteen, he was confirmed into an intention of never again being wrango boy for anybody, not ever.

But when my chance came, I got away from the ranch, too, looking for a way to be someone else than who I had learned to be, someone who was not the owner's kid—and that slick-faced youngster, his yellow shirt and his hair wetted down, glaring at me, got away to go rodeoing, and he was mildly famous for a while. Right then in America, at least in Lake County, the high desert country of Oregon, what all of us young boys wanted was escape and connection with the Great World we had just begun hearing about.

OVER AT THE DOHERTY PLACE in Guano Valley, where we threw all the food down the well that afternoon in 1945, there is a raggedy pale oilcloth tacked to the bullpen walls. On it are written lists of names. Ross Dollarhide, Ernest Messner, Casper Gunderson, Hugh Cahill, Cliff Gunderson—maybe even Tom Anderson, who is cow boss at the IL these days. The lists began back before World War II: the names of men who rode for the MC. The lists are fading out pretty badly now. Half of the men are dead.

Heroes are defined as individuals who go out into the world, leaving home on some kind of quest, endure certain trials of initiation, and come home changed, seeing the world in a fresh way, bearing the wisdom of their experience as news that serves the stay-at-homes in their efforts toward making sense of themselves and of what they are attempting to make of their lives.

In my boyhood we all dreamed of going away to such heroism. And now it looks like things have changed. People are staying home, in that part of the country where they know how to live and what to care about. In some large blurry sense, there no longer seems to be too much currency in the idea that going away to seek your fortune is any sensible road toward anything that matters. Nobody imagines that either the Beatles or big-time rodeoing will save your life.

Not long ago some Hollywood people came out and shot part of a TV special starring Kenny Rogers up there in the Columbia Basin east of the IL. Sounds like it was fine for everybody, all the buckaroos getting in on the camera time and fun and action, but so far nobody has left for Los Angeles with acting on his mind.

Maybe it's just that the world has changed another turn, and life on the high desert looks better than it did in the old days. Maybe the wages are not much, but the food is fine. In my childhood, canned tomatoes all around was a big deal. At the IL wagon, the noontime I was there, they were finishing up with apple and raisin pie about three inches deep. An old-timer named Harold Smith was eating it with sweet canned milk. In that life you learn to wait for simple, specific pleasures.

After scraping their plates, they all went out to the rope corral and climbed up aboard their afternoon horses, which had been caught before the meal in a ceremony that must be ancient among horseback people—one man, the boss, in the center with a riata catching horses with names like Snowball and Snuffy, and each rider choosing his from the string. The white called Snowball was a trifle skittish, crow-hopping a little before he settled down. Then they rode away to another sweep across the sagebrush desert, another branding that afternoon. And I would have liked to have been along as they drifted away to their work, riding unhurriedly into the distance and into an old horseback turn of life in which you can find some pride.

Natural Causes

BARTON LAKE, OREGON: the last of the round barns, the broad conical roof shingled with new cedar, floats on the undulating wheat grass, inhabited by what is gone, that other country where our old people once lived with their horses.

We listen to this hard voice form back then: *You take raw colts just off the desert, and just as wild as a horse can get. You could work with colts in there in the wintertime, when there wasn't much else doing but cows to feed. In there it was like a big circus tent, see.*

The little man from California, Peter French, had two of these barns built in the years 1888 and 1889, when his hold on his great properties—the hay lands of Blitzen and Diamond Valleys and the rising high summer rangeland on Steens Mountain—looked to be most secure. This one is owned and maintained by the Oregon Historical Society.

The other barn, up the valley at the old P Ranch Headquarters, was torn down for materials some fifty years ago: *You got them colts inside, and you went in there with a helper, and your helper would get them going so you could pick up their front feet. We roped them by the front feet, and you threw them down by the front feet. You had to stay careful but the work got done.*

Peter French was beyond a doubt a hard and self-serving man, but he also built his barns from his notion of things done right, to clear artistic proportion and for a purpose, which was the gentling of horses, another beauty. A man of small stature, 5½-half-feet tall and never more than 135 pounds, Peter French ruled all this Steens Mountain and

Blitzen River country of southeastern Oregon when he died in 1897, and he lived only forty-nine years.

We wonder about his intentions for the years he must have seen before him on that day after Christmas, when he was shot and killed while working cattle out in the snowy fields south of the Sod House. We try to speculate on his secrets and see them in the round barn at Barton Lake.

The board-and-batten exterior wall is the first circle. Inside that, with a track between them, is a fortlike circular wall of native stone, nine feet high and maybe two feet thick, cut with portholes and two gates to let in the horses and the reflected light of the sun. There are old-timers in the country who insist the wall was built as defense against attack by Paiute and Bannock tribes. But those natives were mostly gone by then, trapped by military from Idaho Territory operating out of Fort Harney after the uprising of 1878, and trailed north through the terrible January of 1879 to the reservation at Fort Simcoe, southwest of Yakima in Washington Territory. Maybe that rock wall was just meant to be there a long time, or maybe it was intended as a fort against other white men who were coming new and empty-handed into the country. In any event, it is the main structural support of the building.

Opening one of the gates through the wall, we're deep inside and into the space where the men broke horses. This business of entering through circles is part of what we have come to experience. There are two more rings. The first consists of thirteen large juniper posts that support the roof, each sixteen feet out from the center post, a freakishly enormous and smooth-worn peeled juniper that reaches up most of thirty feet to the peak of the conical roof.

Try to imagine roping colts by their front feet, and the harm that must have been possible. High up in what seems a radiant and unnatural light the rafters come to meet at their apex like spokes in a wheel that is not turning. The juniper posts are glowing and golden and look burnished. Some of this aura is no doubt contributed by our imaginations and memories of sunlight coming down through forest trees.

Here, inside, men worked through the boredom of winter with their animals, fighting away the spookiness of isolation amid the flatland sagebrush bluffs near the eastern side of Barton Lake, some fifteen miles of sagebrush and rockflat from the southern edge of Malheur Lake, where newcomers were settling on the mudflats and trying to farm their grain. We wonder about rock walls and Peter French and how much he foresaw, and why he wasn't smart enough to bring peace into the country and save himself from that approaching winter afternoon when Ed Oliver rode toward him across the frozen meadows.

At the beginning Pete French was a kid from Red Bluff, California, who went down the Sacramento River to work in the Willows country for his father's old trail-driving and westering friend, Doctor Hugh Glenn. That was in 1870, the year Peter French was twenty-one and weary of his father's sheep-farmer life.

In the spring of 1872, when Peter French was twenty-three, Hugh Glenn entrusted him with 1,200 head of white and roan shorthorn cattle, six vaqueros, and a Chinese cook, and sent them off trailing north to the almost literally uninhabited high desert rangeland of southeastern Oregon. There were John Devine over at the Whitehorse Ranch where he had settled in 1869, some trappers around the Sod House on the southern edge of Malheur Lake, the military at Fort Harney, miners beyond the Idaho border at Silver City, and the Central Pacific to the south at Winnemucca in Nevada. The frontier was closing back on its remnants, and

Peter French was riding to some of the last empty country, where he found oasis lands that became his true homestake in the world.

The long string of French's herd trailed across the south end of Warner Valley and headed out through the breaks south of the Beatty Buttes and across the fine bunch-grass country of Catlow Valley while Steens Mountain to the east was still bright with snow. Tiny yellow and orange flowers bloomed amid the lava rocks and stunted sage. French had been on the trail two months. He camped at Roaring Springs, resting his cattle on good water and grazing, and while there bought his brand from a man named Porter, the most natural brand imaginable for Pete French, a huge P on the left hip, and the first thing Hugh Glenn was to own in Oregon. The P Ranch was started.

Porter's few head of cattle came with the brand, and so did the land where he grazed, from Roaring Springs to the upper valley of the Donner und Blitzen River. Usage determined right of control in those beginning days. French rode north out of Catlow Valley, over the break at the northwest foot of the Steens, and saw his heartland for the first time: the Blitzen Valley.

French sat horseback on a lava-rock ridge, fifteen hundred feet above the swampy creekside lands reaching north in a long meander as far as he could see, and open for the taking, hay meadows for all the cattle the country could graze, and good water through the year. This great sheltered valley would be his home until he was killed; it held him when leaving would have been easier, when he could have retreated to California and been simple and rich. We imagine Peter French stepping down form his horse and standing there quiet while recognizing the only place where he would fit like a lost piece into a puzzle.

On a knoll near the Blitzen River, French built his willow-thatch corrals and eventually planted his Lombardy poplar and built his white saw-lumber house, where no woman ever lived with him for more than a few days at a time.

A complex history ensued. By 1878 French was selling four-year-old steers at the railhead in Winnemucca. In 1883 he traveled to San Francisco and married Hugh Glenn's daughter, Ella. Sixteen days after the February wedding Hugh Glenn was shot and murdered by an ex-bookkeeper, Huram Miller, and the money troubles began. The estate was valued at $1,232,000 and all of it was encumbered by debt. Peter and Ella French got word at the railroad station in Winnemucca and turned back for the funeral. Ella never attempted returning to the ranch in Oregon. In 1891 they were divorced. By that time it could not have made much difference. The cleanly defined purposes of that young man on horseback, come with other men to claim territory, were deeply muddied while never forgotten.

Hugh Glenn was murdered because he had been cheating his field hands of their wages, in order to pay for a high life with politicians in San Fancisco. Ella gave birth to a son that Peter never claimed in any fatherly way, or so it seems if we look for scandal. The ranchlands in Oregon supported the failures in California and the lawyers. And another battle was taking shape by that time, beginning with the cyclical patterns of rainfall and centering in the ambitions of men come late to the country. It started with one small and at least partly natural event.

FRENCH HAD COME to the Blitzen Valley during dry years, which accounts for the fact that he was able to take hay off the swamplands that first autumn. By the late years of the 1870s he was building drainage canals. Malheur Lake, where the Donner und Blitzen River drained at the far northern end of the P Ranch property, began to refill, and the waters began lapping at the sand reef that had blown in across the overflow channel into landlocked Harney Lake and the alkaline flats on westward.

During the late spring of 1881 the reef washed out, helped a little by human interventions according to stories, and Malheur Lake was lowered, maybe as much as a foot. Almost 10,000 acres of lake-bottom lands were exposed, most of them adjacent to the 1877 meander line that marked the boundaries of the P Ranch. The event did not seem of particular consequence at the time, until settlers began coming into the Harney Basin, looking for lands they could farm. They naturally drifted to the floodplain, which was level and open and inviting to plow. Those families from far away to the east must have thought they had finally come to the reward their suffering had always promised.

And the trouble began: an old Western story, called nesters and ranchers. Under English common law the owner of shoreland is given ownership to the middle or center thread of a stream or lake, in accordance with the doctrine of riparian rights. But Peter French did not know about such rights. The settlers filtered onto the lake-bed lands without opposition until August of 1894, when French returned from consultations with his lawyers and the heirs of the Glenn estate, now determined to see the settlers evicted from the land that legally belonged to the company. French immediately sent letters requesting the settlers to vacate "further occupancy of said lands." The settlers paid the letters little notice, and French brought suit in the Federal court in Portland. The suits were transferred to the Harney County Circuit Court at Burns, and time passed while relations between French and the settlers steadily deteriorated.

Here's where the stories of warfare begin. Alva Springer, one of the settlers, told of being shot at by French's workmen. Springer carried a rifle and galloped beyond the range of their .45 caliber revolvers, climbed down off his horse and put them to flight. "Put a stop to it real soon," was what he said. The only injury was a .45 bullet in a front hoof of the horse he was riding.

Another settler, Al Rienaman, told of Peter French's coming by in a buggy while he was repairing a gate. "Mr. Rienaman," French said, "it's time I gave you a good whipping." French got down from the buggy with the whip he used on his horses and found himself staring down the open end of a revolver. "Mr. Rienaman," he said, "I'll postpone this job until another time." French got back into his buggy and drove on.

Whatever, we hear the anger in these legends of the country, which are still told. The settlers held meetings, hired lawyers, and joined together in a war to save their homes from the baronial power of the P Ranch, which was Peter French and the distant, no doubt rich, California heirs of the Glenn estate.

French's suit finally came to court on May 24, 1897, with Alva Springer as defendant. By that time the P Ranch properties, including the 42,000 acres of pastural hay land in the Diamond Valley that French bought for a dollar an acre in 1877, amounted to 70,000 acres of mostly irrigated meadows. The summer grazing lands that French used as his own in Catlow Valley and on the highlands of Steens amounted to perhaps another million acres.

Local sympathies are easy to imagine. Business men in Burns needed the money and trade brought by the settlers, and poor men on homestead claims all over eastern Oregon were rooting for the settlers. Times were thin. The jury in Burns decided in favor of the defendant, and hatreds ran deeper when it was learned that French was appealing the case. And quite possibly, in any strict reading of the law,

French was right. The land was his, or was until a new meander line was surveyed in 1895, leaving a strip of government land a mile or more wide between French and riparian rights to the shoreline of Malheur Lake. In any event, the settlers were desperate, and angry, as was French. Horse herds were run off, leaving women and children afoot, no small thing in that country. Fences were cut, miles of P Ranch fence, and haystacks were burned. A haze of smoke hung over the Blitzen Valley through half the summer.

There were rumors of gangs and conspiracy. French met with the settlers. "I'll fight any man," he said. "Gentlemen, while this case is pending, come work for me. You can work long as you want and pay for your land." But they did not.

We sense French's division in such talk. Old-timers in the country still speculate about the split in his personality. The people who worked for him were most often enormously loyal, while those in his way were run down by any means possible. We wonder at the attractiveness of those old slate-eyed citizens like French, trying to hold the world to patterns fixed only in their heads.

A story made the rounds. The homesteaders had met and agreed that French must be killed. They had drawn straws for the duty and honor. Somewhere in Harney County there walked a man who had drawn the short straw, and the right to a holy mission of heroism: Kill Peter French. The only sensible way was to shoot him. Everybody wondered who was packing the short straw. And nobody knew if there was any truth in the story.

But they believed Rye Smith. He was a man you could believe. Rye Smith came to the country about the same time as French, and he owned a place in the Diamond Valley and wouldn't sell to French. One evening at the end of a party, while Rye and his wife were gathering their sleeping children from a bedroom, George Miller tried to take a knife to Smith. Rye shot him, the bullet passing through Miller's mouth and out the side of his cheek. Afterward, the two became friends, and Miller confessed. That night with the knife . . . he had been hired to kill. Peter French had done the hiring. These are stories you hear, which isn't to say they are true or not. They were true enough.

ED OLIVER WAS A MAN of small stature, like Peter French, six inches short of six feet tall, a homesteader on property one mile south of Rockford Lane, a public road running east and west through French's property in the Blitzen Valley, and he had his history of violence and his grievances. In the fall of 1894 Oliver had been charged with assault with a dangerous weapon. He'd beat on Sam Hadley with a long-handled shovel and been indicted, but the case was finally dropped.

Oliver's homestead land was located inside French's boundary fence, and French demanded $500 for a right of way to Rockford Lane, money Oliver couldn't pay, and probably would not have paid if he could. French threatened him publicly. "I'll fix you good if I ever catch you on my property." Or some such warning.

Oliver was married to Ida Simmons, whose parents lived on the shoreline of Malheur Lake, settlers on land Peter French claimed was his by riparian right. She had lost her first husband and was left with four children and a few cows. Ignoring French's warning, Oliver took the cows to the homestead south of Rockford Lane, leaving Ida and her children with her mother.

On Christmas morning, 1897, Oliver traveled to Malheur Lake and spent the day with his family, and we have to conjecture about his holiday. Times were thin, and Ed Oliver had his grievances, which carried weight greater than rumors of childish pacts and grown men drawing straws like playground brats.

French came back from Chicago on Christmas Day of 1897, a windy Christmas morning with snow blowing in the streets of Burns, and he bundled himself and his gifts from the east into a buggy-wagon and spent the cold day driving the thirty miles south to the Sod House, where his riders were camped. Peter French didn't spend much time around the establishments in Burns, not in those days. You had to wonder how he was feeling. All the trouble with lawyers, and his wife divorced and married to another man in San Francisco, and the fourteen-year-old boy who bore his name, spoiled and self-centered and redheaded and not looking anything like French—all of them wanting money and none of them any help when it came to the work.

You had to think French carried his own grievances that morning after Christmas. There had been a party the night before at the Sod House, his ranch crew with all their children and women, and the next day there was Chino Berdugo, the cow boss, down with too much holiday, which was surely understandable. French told Chino to take the buckboard and team and go upriver to the P Ranch headquarters and rest for a day.

Now the stories get more contradictory. Toward noon, we hear, French cut himself a willow switch and tied a strap of buckskin on it, making a little whip. They were moving 3,000 head of cattle that day, and it was slow going. Around two o'clock in the afternoon French rode ahead and threw open the gate between the Big Sagebrush Field and the Wright Field.

We know roughly what comes next, and we watch French turn the stirrup and get himself horseback on Chino's sorrel gelding, and we are not surprised when Ed Oliver comes riding hard from a snowy draw, where the dry snow flies in wispy clouds blown by the wind of his traveling, Ed Oliver coming hard and spurring like a man with news that cannot wait. Ed Oliver came right on and he ran his horse right up into French, banging full in without any try at stopping, like a man gone blind or crazy. French's horse shied backwards and halfway fell. It was a sudden madman thing. Or so it looked. Emanuel Clark was nearby and saw it.

And Emanuel Clark was a man anybody would trust, all his life. Ed Oliver spun his horse and charged French again, and French whipped at him over the head and shoulders with the willow-stick whip. Oliver backed off a few yards and pulled a pistol from his waistband. We can try to see the lucky shot slowly—the two angry men, their horses blowing and frightened, the one inexperienced with his weapon. Oliver raised his pistol and fired.

But there's another version of these events, in which French got a willow stave from the fence and took to beating at Oliver after a harmless gate-side encounter, Oliver who was riding a workhorse and didn't have much chance of getting away.

In this version, after taking a few blows to the head and shoulders, Oliver pulled his .32 caliber revolver and fired one shot from a total of three in the cylinder. The shot hit French above the eye. They were two hundred yards from the gate when this occurred.

In both versions, against any imaginable odds, the bullet explodes from beneath Peter French's left ear, and the history of that country is marked by a turning. The fragments of bone and the blood hang in the cold winter air with time stopped as everything changes. We try to hear the little popping of the pistol in the wind, and see Peter French already dead as he falls, and Oliver spurring his horse and riding away into his escape from what has happened.

Doctor Volk, who examined Oliver the next day, stated that Oliver had a dislocated thumb and severe bruises on the right side of his head and shoulders. We wonder if these injuries could have been inflicted by a willow stick with a piece of buckskin tied to the end of it.

The body was left where it fell, covered with some saddle blankets until nightfall, when Andrea Littrell came out from the Sod House where he worked and set up a tent. David Crow was another man like Emanuel Clark who was to live a long life in the country after French's death, retelling what he saw, and a hero because of the famous ride he began later—changing horses at the headquarters of the P Ranch and carrying the word, changing horses nine times before he reached Winnemucca in forty-three hours without resting.

The Harney County Coroner, T. W. Stephens, took charge of French's body the next day and transported it to the living quarters of Leon Brown in Burns, where Doctor W. L. Marsden conducted his investigation. Death by gunshot.

The body was placed in a zinc-lined box and shipped by wagon to Baker City, where it was embalmed and shipped on by Wells Fargo Express to Red Bluff, where Peter French was buried alongside his father and mother in the Oak Hill Cemetery on January 4, 1898.

The trial of Ed Oliver took place on May 19, 1898, in Burns. After various partisan and contradictory testimony a jury of his peers stayed out three hours before returning a verdict of *not guilty*. On October 11 of that same year Oliver's wife divorced him, and Oliver vanishes from the records of a country where the good parts were by then vividly mapped in bright colors and mostly settled. Some say he left with a woman, others say he was killed by P Ranch cowboys—but in any event he was gone from that other republic where our old people lived with their horses and the natural consequences of their ambitions, their dreams of constructing one perfect round barn in which to work through the winter months, to which we are the heirs apparent.

Burning It All

IMAGINE THE SLOW HISTORY of our country in the far reaches of southeastern Oregon, a backlands enclave even in the American West, the first settlers not arriving until a decade after the end of the Civil War. I've learned to think of myself as having had the luck to grow up at the tail end of a way of existing in which people lived in everyday proximity to animals on territory they knew more precisely than the patterns in the palms of their hands.

In Warner Valley we understood our property as others know their cities, a landscape of neighborhoods, some sacred, some demonic, some habitable, some not, which is as the sea, they tell me, is understood by fishermen. It was only later, in college, that I learned it was possible to understand Warner as a fertile oasis in a vast featureless sagebrush desert.

Over in that other world on the edge of rain-forests which is the Willamette Valley of Oregon, I'd gone to school in General Agriculture, absorbed in a double-bind sort of learning, studying to center myself in the County Agent/ Corps of Engineers mentality they taught and at the same time taking classes from Bernard Malamud and wondering with great romantic fervor if it was in me to write the true history of the place where I had always lived.

Straight from college I went to Photo Intelligence work in the Air Force. The last couple of those years were spent deep in jungle on the island of Guam, where we lived in a little compound of cleared land, in a Quonset hut.

The years on Guam were basically happy and bookish: we were newly married, with children. A hundred or so yards

north of our Quonset hut, along a trail through the luxuri-
ant undergrowth between coconut palms and banana trees,
a ragged cliff of red porous volcanic rock fell directly to the
ocean. When the Pacific typhoons came roaring in, our hut
was washed with blowing spray from the great breakers.
On calm days we would stand on the cliff at that absolute
edge of our jungle and island and gaze out across to the island of Rota, and to the endlessness of ocean beyond, and I
would marvel at my life, so far from southeastern Oregon.

And then in the late fall of 1958, after I had been gone
from Warner Valley for eight years, I came back to participate in our agriculture. The road in had been paved, we had
Bonneville Power on lines from the Columbia River, and
high atop the western rim of the valley there was a TV
translator, which beamed fluttering pictures from New York
and Los Angeles direct to us.

And I had changed, or thought I had, for a while. No
more daydreams about writing the true history. Try to understand my excitement as I climbed to the rim behind our
house and stood there by our community TV translator.
The valley where I had always seen myself living was open
before me like another map and playground, and this time I
was an adult, and high up in the War Department. Looking
down maybe 3,000 feet into Warner, and across to the high
basin and range desert where we summered our cattle, I
saw the beginnings of my real life as an agricultural man-
ager. The flow of watercourses in the valley was spread before me like a map, and I saw it as a surgeon might see the
flow of blood across a chart of anatomy, and saw myself
helping to turn the fertile homeplace of my childhood into
a machine for agriculture whose features could be delineated with the same surgeon's precision in my mind.

It was work that can be thought of as craftsmanlike,
both artistic and mechanical, creating order according to an

ideal of beauty based on efficiency, manipulating the forces of water and soil, season and seed, manpower and equipment, laying out functional patterns for irrigation and cultivation on the surface of our valley. We drained and leveled, ditched and pumped, and for a long while our crops were all any of us could have asked. There were over 5,000 water control devices. We constructed a perfect agricultural place, and it was sacred, so it seemed.

~

AGRICULTURE IS OFTEN ENVISIONED as an art, and it can be. Of course there is always survival, and bank notes, and all that. But your basic bottom line on the farm is again and again some notion of how life should be lived. The majority of agricultural people, if you press them hard enough, even though most of them despise sentimental abstractions, will admit they are trying to create a good place, and to live as part of that goodness, in the kind of connection which with fine reason we call *rootedness*. It's just that there is good art and bad art.

These are thoughts which come back when I visit eastern Oregon. I park and stand looking down into the lava-rock and juniper-tree canyon where Deep Creek cuts its way out of the Warner Mountains, and the great turkey buzzard soars high in the yellow-orange light above the evening. The fishing water is low, as it always is in late August, unfurling itself around dark and broken boulders. The trout, I know, are hanging where the currents swirl across themselves, waiting for the one entirely precise and lucky cast, the Renegade fly bobbing toward them.

Even now I can see it, each turn of water along miles of that creek. Walk some stretch enough times with a fly rod and its configurations will imprint themselves on your being with Newtonian exactitude. Which is beyond doubt

one of the attractions of such fishing—the hours of learning, and then the intimacy with a living system that carries
you beyond the sadness of mere gaming for sport.

What I liked to do, back in the old days, was pack in
some spuds and an onion and corn flour and spices mixed
up in a plastic bag, a small cast-iron frying pan in my wicker
creel and, in the late twilight on a gravel bar by the water,
cook up a couple of rainbows over a fire of snapping dead
willow and sage, eating alone while the birds flitted through
the last hatch, wiping my greasy fingers on my pants while
the heavy trout began rolling at the lower ends of the pools.

The canyon would be shadowed under the moon when I
walked out to show up home empty-handed, to sit with my
wife over a drink of whiskey at the kitchen table. Those
nights I would go to bed and sleep without dreams, a grown-
up man secure in the house and the western valley where he
had been a child, enclosed in a topography of spirit he as-
sumed he knew more closely than his own features in the
shaving mirror.

So, I ask myself, if it was such a pretty life, why didn't I
stay? The peat soil in Warner Valley was deep and rich, we
ran good cattle, and my most sacred memories are centered
there. What could run me off?

Well, for openers, it got harder and harder to get out
of bed in the mornings and face the days, for reasons I
didn't understand. More and more I sought the comfort of
fishing that knowable creek. Or in winter the blindness of
television.

My father grew up on a homestead place on the sagebrush flats outside Silver Lake, Oregon. He tells of hiding
under the bed with his sisters when strangers came to the
gate. He grew up, as we all did in that country and era, believing that the one sure defense against the world was
property. I was born in 1932 and recall a life before the end

of World War II in which it was possible for a child to imagine that his family owned the world.

Warner Valley was largely swampland when my grandfather bought the MC Ranch with no down payment in 1936, right at the heart of the Great Depression. The outside work was done mostly by men and horses and mules, and our ranch valley was filled with life. In 1937 my father bought his first track-layer, a secondhand RD6 Caterpillar he used to build a 17-mile diversion canal to carry the spring floodwater around the east side of the valley, and we were on our way to draining all swamps. The next year he bought an RD7 and a John Deere 36 combine that cut an 18-foot swath, and we were deeper into the dream of power over nature and men, which I had begun to inhabit while playing those long-ago games of war.

The peat ground left by the decaying remnants of ancient tule beds was diked into huge undulating grain fields—Houston Swamp with 750 irrigated acres, Dodson Lake with 800—a final total of almost 8,000 acres under cultivation, and for reasons of what seemed like common sense and efficiency, the work became industrialized. Our artistry worked toward a model whose central image was the machine.

The natural patterns of drainage were squared into dragline ditches, the tules and the aftermath of the oat and barley crops were burned—along with a little more of the combustible peat soil every year. We flood-irrigated when the water came in spring, drained in late March, and planted in a 24-hour-a-day frenzy that began around April 25 and ended—with luck—by the 10th of May, just as leaves on the Lombardy poplar were breaking from their buds. We summered our cattle on more than a million acres of Taylor Grazing Land across the high lava-rock and sagebrush desert out east of the valley, miles of territory where we owned most of what water there was, and it was ours. We owned it all, or so we felt. The government was as distant as news on the radio.

The most intricate part of my job was called "balancing water," a night and day process of opening and closing pipes and redwood headgates and running the 18-inch drainage pumps. That system was the finest plaything I ever had.

And despite the mud and endless hours, the work remained play for a long time, the making of a thing both functional and elegant. We were doing God's labor and creating a good place on earth, living the pastoral yeoman dream— that's how our mythology defined it, although nobody would ever have thought to talk about work in that way.

And then it all went dead, over years, but swiftly.

You can imagine our surprise and despair, our sense of having been profoundly cheated. It took us a long while to realize some unnamable thing was wrong, and then we blamed it on ourselves, our inability to manage enough. But the fault wasn't ours, beyond the fact that we had all been educated to believe in a grand bad factory-land notion as our prime model of excellence.

We felt enormously betrayed. For so many years, through endless efforts, we had proceeded in good faith, and it turned out we had wrecked all we had not left untouched. The beloved migratory rafts of waterbirds, the green-headed mallards and the redheads and canvasbacks, the cinnamon teal and the great Canadian honkers, were mostly gone along with their swampland habitat. The hunting, in so many ways, was no longer what it had been.

We wanted to build a reservoir, and litigation started. Our laws were being used against us, by people who wanted a share of what we thought of as our water. We could not endure the boredom of our mechanical work and couldn't hire anyone who cared enough to do it right. We baited the coyotes with 1080, and rodents destroyed our alfalfa; we

sprayed weeds and insects with 2-4-D Ethyl and Mala-
thion, and Parathion for clover mite, and we shortened our
own lives.

In quite an actual way we had come to victory in the
artistry of our playground warfare against all that was naturally alive in our native home. We had reinvented our valley according to the most persuasive ideal given us by our
culture, and we ended with a landscape organized like a
machine for growing crops and fattening cattle, a machine
that creaked a little louder each year, a dreamland gone
wrong.

One of my strongest memories comes from a morning
when I was maybe ten years old, out on the lawn before our
country home in spring, beneath a bluebird sky. I was
watching the waterbirds coming off the valley swamps and
grain fields where they had been feeding overnight. They
were going north to nesting grounds on the Canadian tundra, and that piece of morning, inhabited by the sounds of
their wings and their calling in the clean air, was wonder-
filled and magical. I was enclosed in a living place.

No doubt that memory has persisted because it was a
sight of possibility that I will always cherish—an image
of the great good place rubbed smooth over the years like
a river stone, which I touch again as I consider why life in
Warner Valley went so seriously haywire. But never again
in my lifetime will it be possible for a child to stand out on
a bright spring morning in Warner Valley and watch the
waterbirds come through in enormous, rafting vee-shaped
flocks of thousands—and I grieve.

My father is a very old man. A while back we were driving up the Bitterroot Valley of Montana, and he was gazing
away to the mountains. "They'll never see it the way we
did," he said, and I wonder what he saw.

We shaped our piece of the West according to the model

provided by our mythology, and instead of a great good place such order had given us enormous power over nature and a blank perfection of fields.

~

A MYTHOLOGY CAN BE UNDERSTOOD as a story that contains a set of implicit instructions from a society to its members, telling them what is valuable and how to conduct themselves if they are to preserve the things they value.

The teaching mythology we grew up with in the American West is a pastoral story of agricultural ownership. The story begins with a vast innocent continent, natural and almost magically alive, capable of inspiring us to reverence and awe, and yet savage, a wilderness. A good rural people come from the East, and they take the land from its native inhabitants, and tame it for agricultural purposes, bringing civilization: a notion of how to live embodied in law. The story is as old as invading armies, and at heart it is a racist, sexist, imperialist mythology of conquest; a rationale for violence—against other people and against nature.

At the same time, that mythology is a lens through which we continue to see ourselves. Many of us like to imagine ourselves as honest yeomen who sweat and work in the woods or the mines or the fields for a living. And many of us are. We live in a real family, a work-centered society, and we like to see ourselves as people with the good luck and sense to live in a place where some vestige of the natural world still exists in working order. Many of us hold that natural world as sacred to some degree, just as it is in our myth. Lately, more and more of us are coming to understand our society in the American West as an exploited colony, threatened by greedy outsiders who want to take our sacred place away from us, or at least to strip and degrade it.

In short, we see ourselves as a society of mostly decent

people who live with some connection to a holy wilderness, threatened by those who lust for power and property. We look for Shane to come riding out of the Tetons, and instead we see Exxon and the Sierra Club. One looks virtually as alien as the other.

And our mythology tells us we own the West, absolutely and morally—we own it because of our history. Our people brought law to this difficult place, they suffered and they shed blood and they survived, and they earned this land for us. Our efforts have surely earned us the right to absolute control over the thing we created. The myth tells us this place is ours, and will always be ours, to do with as we see fit.

That's a most troubling and enduring message, because we want to believe it, and we do believe it, so many of us, despite its implicit ironies and wrongheadedness, despite the fact that we took the land from someone else. We try to ignore a genocidal history of violence against the Native Americans.

In the American West we are struggling to revise our dominant mythology, and to find a new story to inhabit. Laws control our lives, and they are designed to preserve a model of society based on values learned from mythology. Only after re-imagining our myths can we coherently re-model our laws, and hope to keep our society in a realistic relationship to what is actual.

In Warner Valley we thought we were living the right lives, creating a great precise perfection of fields, and we found the mythology had been telling us an enormous lie. The world had proven too complex, or the myth too simple-minded. And we were mortally angered.

The truth is, we never owned all the land and water. We don't even own very much of them, privately. And we don't own anything absolutely or forever. As our society grows more and more complex and interwoven, our entitlement becomes less and less absolute, more and more likely to be legally diminished. Our rights to property will never take precedence over the needs of society. Nor should they, we all must agree in our grudging hearts. Ownership of property has always been a privilege granted by society, and revokable.

~

DOWN BY THE SLAUGHTERHOUSE my grandfather used to keep a chicken-wire cage for trapping magpies. The cage was as high as a man's head and mounted on a sled so it could be towed off and cleaned. It worked on the same principle as a lobster trap. Those iridescent black-and-white birds could get in to feed on the intestines of butchered cows—we never butchered a fat heifer or steer for our own consumption, only aged dry cows culled from the breeding herd—but they couldn't get out.

Trapped under the noontime sun, the magpies would flutter around in futile exploration for a while and then would give in to a great sullen presentiment of their fate, just hopping around and picking at leftovers and waiting.

My grandfather was Scots-English and a very old man by then, but his blue eyes never turned watery and lost. He was one of those cowmen we don't see so often anymore, heedless of most everything outside his playground, which was livestock and seasons and property, and, as the seasons turned, more livestock and more property, a game that could be called accumulation.

All the notes were paid off, and you would have thought my grandfather would have been secure and released to ease back in wisdom.

But no such luck. It seemed he had to keep proving his ownership. This took various forms, like endless litigation, which I have heard described as the sport of kings, but the manifestation I recall most vividly was that of killing magpies.

In the summer the ranch hands would butcher in the after-supper cool of an evening a couple of times a week. About once a week, when a number of magpies had gathered in the trap, maybe 10 or 15, my grandfather would get out his lifetime 12-gauge shotgun and have someone drive him down to the slaughterhouse in his dusty, ancient gray Cadillac, so he could look over his catch and get down to the business at hand. Once there, the ritual was slow and dignified, and always inevitable as one shoe after another.

The old man would sit there a while in his Cadillac and gaze at the magpies with his merciless blue eyes, and the birds would stare back with their hard black eyes. The summer dust would settle around the Cadillac, and the silent confrontation would continue. It would last several minutes.

Then my grandfather would sigh, swing open the door on his side of the Cadillac, and climb out, dragging his shotgun behind him, the pockets of his gray gabardine suit-coat like a frayed uniform bulging with shells. The stock of the shotgun had been broken sometime deep in the past, and it was wrapped with fine brass wire, which shone golden in the sunlight while the old man thumbed shells into the magazine. All this without saying a word.

In the ear of my mind I try to imagine the radio playing softly in the Cadillac, something like "Room Full of Roses" or "Candy Kisses," but there was no radio. There was just the ongoing hum of insects and the clacking of the mechanism as the old man pumped a shell into the firing chamber.

He would lift the shotgun, and from no more than twelve feet, sighting down that barrel where the bluing was mostly worn off, through the chicken wire into the eyes of those trapped magpies, he would kill them one by one, taking his time, maybe so as to prove that this was no accident.

He would fire and there would be a minor explosion of blood and feathers, the huge booming of the shotgun echoing through the flattening light of early afternoon, off the sage-covered hills and down across the hay meadows and the sloughs lined with dagger-leafed willow, frightening great flights of blackbirds from fence lines nearby, to rise in flocks and wheel and be gone.

"Bastards," my grandfather would mutter, and then he would take his time about killing another, and finally he would be finished and turn without looking back, and climb into his side of the Cadillac, where the door still stood open. Whoever it was whose turn it was that day would drive him back up the willow-lined lane through the meadows to the ranch house beneath the Lombardy poplar, to the cool shaded living room with its faded linoleum where the old man would finish out his day playing pinochle with my grandmother and anyone else he could gather, sometimes taking a break to retune a favorite program on the Zenith Trans-Oceanic radio.

No one in our family, so far as I ever heard, knew any reason why the old man had come to hate magpies with such specific intensity in his old age. The blackbirds were endlessly worse, the way they would mass together in flocks of literally thousands, to strip and thrash in his oat and barley fields, and then feed all fall in the bins of grain stockpiled to fatten his cattle.

"Where is the difference?" I asked him once, about the magpies.

"Because they're mine," he said. I never did know exactly what he was talking about, the remnants of entrails left over from the butchering of culled stocker cows, or the magpies. But it became clear he was asserting his absolute lordship over both, and over me, too, so long as I was living on his property. For all his life and most of mine the notion of property as absolute seemed like law, even when it never was.

Most of us who grew up owning land in the West believed that any impairment of our right to absolute control of that property was a taking, forbidden by the so-called "taking clause" of the Constitution. We believed regulation of our property rights could never legally reduce the value of our property. After all, what was the point of ownership if it was not profitable? Any infringement on the control of private property was a communist perversion.

But all over the West, as in all of America, the old folkway of property as an absolute right is dying. Our mythology doesn't work anymore.

We find ourselves weathering a rough winter of discontent, snared in the uncertainties of a transitional time and urgently yearning to inhabit a story that might bring sensible order to our lives—even as we know such a story can only evolve through an almost literally infinite series of recognitions of what, individually, we hold sacred. The liberties our people came seeking are more and more constrained, and here in the West, as everywhere, we hate it.

Simple as that. And we have to live with it. There is no more running away to territory. This is it, for most of us. We have no choice but to live in community. If we're lucky we may discover a story that teaches us to abhor our old romance with conquest and possession.

My grandfather died in 1958, toppling out of his chair at the pinochle table, soon after I came back to Warner, but his vision dominated our lives until we sold the ranch in 1967. An ideal of absolute ownership that defines family as property is the perfect device for driving people away from one another. There was a rule in our family. "What's good for the property is good for you."

"Every time there was more money we bought land," my grandmother proclaimed after learning my grandfather had been elected to the Cowboy Hall of Fame. I don't know if she spoke with pride or bitterness, but I do know that, having learned to understand love as property, we were all absolutely divided at the end; relieved to escape amid a litany of divorce and settlements, our family broken in the getaway.

I cannot grieve for my grandfather. It is hard to imagine, these days, that any man could ever again think he owns the birds.

~~~

THANK THE LORD THERE WERE other old men involved in my upbringing. My grandfather on my mother's side ran away from a Germanic farmstead in Wisconsin the year he was fourteen, around 1900, and made his way to Butte. "I was lucky," he would say. "I was too young to go down in the mines, so they put me to sharpening steel."

Seems to me such a boy must have been lucky to find work at all, wandering the teeming difficult streets of the most urban city in the American West. "Well, no," he said. "They put you to work. It wasn't like that. They were good to me in Butte. They taught me a trade. That's all I did was work. But it didn't hurt me any."

After most of ten years on the hill—broke and on strike, still a very young man—he rode the rails south to the silver mines in what he called "Old Mexico," and then worked his way back north through the mining country of Nevada in time for the glory days in Goldfield and Rhyolite and Tonopah. At least those are the stories he would tell. "This is Las Vegas," he would say. "When I was there you could have bought it all for a hundred and fifty dollars. Cost you ten cents for a drink of water."

To my everlasting sadness, I never really quizzed him on the facts. Now I look at old photographs of those mining camps and wonder. It's difficult for me to imagine the good gentle man I knew walking those tough dusty streets. He belonged, at least in those Butte days, to the International Brotherhood of Blacksmiths and Helpers. I still have his first dues card. He was initiated July 11, 1904, and most of the months of 1904 and 1905 are stamped, DUES PAID.

AL DIED IN AN OLD FOLKS' HOME in Eugene, Oregon. During the days of his last summer, when he knew the jig was up, a fact he seemed to regard with infallible good humor, we would sit in his room and listen to the aged bemused woman across the hall chant her litany of childhood, telling herself that she was somebody and still real.

It was always precisely the same story, word by particular word. I wondered then how much of it was actual, lifting from some deep archive in her memory, and now I wonder how much of it was pure sweet invention, occasioned by the act of storytelling and by the generative, associative power of language. I cannot help but think of ancient fires, light flickering on the faces of children and storytellers detailing the history of their place in the scheme of the earth.

The story itself started with a screen-door slamming and her mother yelling at her when she was a child coming out from the back porch of a white house, and rotting apples on the ground under the trees in the orchard, and a dog that snapped at the flies. "Mother," she would exclaim in exasperation, "I'm fine."

The telling took about three minutes, and she told it like a story for grandchildren. "That's nice," she would say to her dog. "That's nice."

Then she would lapse into quiet, rewinding herself, seeing

an old time when the world contained solace enough to seem complete, and she would start over again, going on until she had lulled herself back into sleep. I would wonder if she was dreaming about that dog amid the fallen apples, snapping at flies and yellowjackets.

At the end she would call the name of that dog over and over in a quavering, beseeching voice—and my grandfather would look to me from his bed and his eyes would be gleaming with laughter, such an old man laughing painfully, his shoulders shaking, and wheezing.

"Son of a bitch," he would whisper, when she was done calling the dog again, and he would wipe the tears from his face with the sleeve of his hospital gown. *Son of a bitch.* He would look to me again, and other than aimless grinning acknowledgment that some mysterious thing was truly funny, I wouldn't know what to do, and then he would look away to the open window, beyond which a far-off lawn mower droned, like this time he was the one who was embarrassed. Not long after that he was dead, and so was the old woman across the hall.

"Son of a bitch," I thought, when we were burying Al one bright afternoon in Eugene, and I found myself suppressing laughter. Maybe it was just a way of ditching my grief for myself, who did not know him well enough to really understand what he thought was funny. I have Al's picture framed on my wall, and I can still look to him and find relief from the old insistent force of my desire to own things. His laughter is like a gift.

Leaving

SAY IT IS LATE FEBRUARY and the winter runoff is just beginning, Deep Creek and Twenty-Mile coming high and muddy from the Warner Mountains. A cold, dark morning, spitting rain, and miles of mudslick levee banks to patrol before breakfast, pumps and head gates to check.

Rotten conditions, you might think, and they were when you fooled around and got yourself stuck before daybreak and had to walk out three miles for help. But swear to God, that wasn't it—I never did run clear out of patience with getting the work done. My reasons for leaving had more to do with what might be called varieties of loneliness.

Some rewards of farming I loved until the day I left. On late May evenings, after supper, with the dishes stacked in the sink, my wife and my son and daughter and I would load into my blue 1961 Ford pickup and drive the ranch roads through the wild meadows and willows along the sloughs where the redwing blackbirds flocked, the occasional teal and mallards with their ducklings in the mossy water—all lovely as the dust settled—to see our crops.

Off west the sun would be low near the rim, which was black against such light, and amid the dark groves of silver poplar and cottonwood the lights shone from our kitchen, and from the homes of people we had neighbored with all our adult lives. For at least that little while we would sense ourselves whole and part of an inhabited place. As we sighted down the drill-rows of barley seedlings—the crop backlit, luminous yellow-green and fragile against the dark, moist soil—it would seem that just this might be enough to sustain us, always.

73

CONSIDER ANOTHER MEMORY, this from the last years of farming, driving our 17-mile levee bank around the east side of the valley in midsummer, as I began to recognize and name the malaise that drove me to leave. On one side the expanse of Houston Swamp was patched yellow and green as the barley ripened toward harvest in late August. On the other side, *the outside* as we called it, there lay an alkaline flatland where the floodwaters backed up from the levee, drowned dead sage and greasewood reaching maybe half a mile to the first rise of the scab rock hillslopes that lengthened into the desert land of northern Nevada. Both the stillness of the field and that expanse of alkali shimmered in the heat, and both were empty.

Leaning on the tailgate of my pickup, I first came to my awareness that this valley where I had always lived had gone lifeless in some terrible way, and I was frightened. No more waterbirds, and most of the neighbors had moved away as the land was consolidated into what jargon calls "feasible economic units," and miles away, dust rose in twisting strings to the sky from behind our half-dozen three-wire New Holland hay balers.

IN HINDSIGHT I CAN SEE that my pilgrimage toward that moment began with my mother. She grew up the daughter of a power company blacksmith in Klamath Falls, and like so many small-town women, she took piano and voice lessons, she was pretty and good at her music, and she yearned not so much to escape as to live a life of consequence. She is an old woman now, and I think that yearning inhabits her yet, driving her to despair. But I bless her, because in the long working-out she passed to me a notion that there was more to life than cattle ranching.

Like so many young people who grow up isolated from

things our culture defines as significant, I felt myself cut off
from the Great World in irrevocable ways, and driven to the
contrary idea that the things I knew were worthless, or at
least of no interest to anybody else, because they were so
private.

In Warner Valley we lived a long way from bookstores.
And I had come to worship and yearn for books and ideas,
nodding my head in dim-witted agreement with Camus,
terrified by *The Magic Mountain,* subscribing to the *New
York Times Book Review,* the *Kenyon Review,* the *Sewanee
Review,* the *Hudson Review,* and the *Virginia Quarterly
Review,* ordering eight or ten deeply serious books a month
long distance from San Francisco, hungering before the
meager collections shelved in stationery stores when I got to
town, a grown man with family, ill-educated and close to
paralyzed by the fact that I no longer wanted any life I
could imagine as possibly mine. My yearnings seemed almost perverse. Why couldn't the immediacy of family and
work and property be enough?

How right and ironic it seemed that afternoon in Shaw's
Stationery in Klamath Falls, as I leafed through a recent
reissue of *Oregon Place Names* and found the name Lonely.
I pitied the poor folks who might live there, and it turned
out to be the former name of Adel, the tiny hamlet in Warner Valley where I had been raised and was living right at
the moment. Not one thing about such a sappish discovery
loomed comic at that time in my life.

Eventually I made other finds in Shaw's Stationery—
Theodore Roethke's *Collected Poems,* for one—and I read,
in "The Far Field":

Among the tin cans, tires, rusted pipes, broken
     machinery,
One learned of the eternal.

The poem goes on to talk about dead rats and tomcats and ground beetles, among specifically named flowers and birds, referring to Roethke's childhood wanderings through his father's greenhouses in Michigan, but I was transfixed right there in Klamath Falls. Roethke's experience in some back corner was valuable if only because he cherished it in such accurate language, and mine might be, someday, maybe. In any event I recognized chances I had to take but could not identify in Roethke, and about then began another version of my life, a story to tell myself and live by. So to hell with it, I thought, I'll be whatever it is I can't quit being. Another romance with myself, as if they all weren't.

By early October of those years in the 1960s our four old John Deere 36 combines had been dragged into a row out behind the Caterpillar shop. The light over the harvested barley fields would come up golden and clean for a couple of dozen perfect days.

The great fault-block of Warner Rim lifted three thousand feet just at my back, marked in long terraces by the remnants of rocky shoreline left behind as some ancient sea dried up. A few miles north, along a thin curve of peninsula reaching out into a shallow floodwater lake, we had found chipped obsidian arrow-points by the bucketful when I was a child. The native peoples must have camped there on these same kinds of limitless fall days, awaiting the calling, undulating rafts of waterbirds, and the good hunting. In my imagination those people were absolutely quiet and at peace with their intentions. For them, things had always been like this.

Archaeologists know of a quarter million points picked up along the shores of Crump Lake, and in the 1940s kids in the country, like me, had a hundred or two stored in a shoe box somewhere. In seasons when the water was low we would wander amid the shredding expanses of dry tule and find the points in clusters of a dozen or more. By the end of World War II, people were out there with shovels and screens, like miners, determined to reap their share of whatever bounty they imagined this was. I knew a man who had half a dozen horse-shoe nail kegs filled with arrowheads in his garage.

By the 1960s the shore of Crump Lake felt too lonesome for anybody in my spiritual condition. The afternoons there didn't seem inhabited anymore. But south along the thread of gravel road there were huge smooth-sided boulders etched with lichen growing along the traces of petroglyph drawings, snakes and sunrises, figures of animals and men, perhaps drawn there in acts of celebration or supplication. Who could know? In any event, the boulders were a truck-load each, and nobody had carried them away to a garage. On fine October days I would study those drawings and wonder what it could have been like to be native in that place where I had come to feel so distant from any hint of proper purpose.

Several hundred feet up the scree slopes, along the ter-raced rocky lines that marked the shores of that ancient sea, there were caves at the foot of the occasional layered lava-rock outcroppings. Nobody I knew had ever climbed up to them, likely because our energies in that valley went mostly to work, and sweating up some scree slope toward those unimpressive thin lines of shadow seemed like such a thun-deringly pointless thing to do. But anybody could see that those old hunting-gathering people who etched their de-signs on the boulders along the road might have sheltered themselves up there, and I was looking for somebody to be. Maybe I could be an intellectual rancher who did bookish things like archaeology on the side.

Such are the stories we tell ourselves. I didn't know any-body like that, but I entertained thoughts of buying the weekly newspaper over in the county seat and being the rancher/newspaper guy who wrote a fascinating column every week with cowshit on his boots. As I say, I felt ruined for the country generosities of the life I had inherited. A good crop of barley was in the bin that fall, and it wasn't enough. So I climbed up to the caves, packing my #2 irrigating shovel.

The rough, sloping roof over the mouth of the shallow cave was black and encrusted, and I had read enough to guess what that meant—soot and animal fats, a long history of cook fires, maybe over centuries. My theories were right, people had sheltered themselves here. I was truly and immediately excited, my hands trembling as I envisioned some great simple goldfield find, trying to put aside my fantastical notions of who I would be now that such impossible bonanza luck had come my way.

What I remember next is the shoveling, there in the mounded rubble at the mouth of the cave, where I had room to stand and work while fighting back the feeling that this was make-believe and not part of my actual life at all. Since the end of harvest I had been searching, unconsciously or not, seeking signs and omens to kick me forward into the process of creating a story of who I should be. Those that I acknowledged had brought me to this hillside above the place where I had always lived, digging for buried secrets. It was a scenario my cattle-rancher friends might understand as literally indicative of craziness. And more than anything I was terrified that they might be right about someone so unmoored from the routines of normal life as it was supposed to be lived in our valley.

But before long my shoveling turned up a reward I at first could not make sense of: a fragment of fine matting woven from rushes. It seemed impossible that the people who drew those cartoon marks on the boulders below could have known how to work so intricately with materials so commonplace in the valley. But connections started forming.

A few miles away, on the flat-topped lava outcroppings along the eastern side of the valley, there were smooth cylindrical holes worn ten or fifteen inches into the fundamental stone by Modoc or Shoshoni or Klamath natives grinding the native grains. The holes are like bowls, and once worked into the outcropping they could not be destroyed by enemies. Whatever tribe it was and how many thousands of hours at the grinding it took to wear those holes no one knows—but for me, like the crumbling woven mat, that stone worn to the shape of the work came to exist as metaphor.

There in the mouth of my shallow cave I realized my connection to the continuities of life in the place where I lived. It was an instant that cannot help but sound soft-headed in the recounting, but I think of it as a quite classical recognition, in which I began to sense the legitimacy of an urge to tell stories.

In some way or another we all do it. You go in any tavern and show any sign of weakness, and some beleaguered soul will start telling you the story of his life. You always feel like you ought to listen, at least for a little while.

We find stories in the unpatterned restlessness of our lives, and in the histories of the places we have lived, and we tell them and retell them, if only to ourselves, living them out and sharpening and reinventing them, discovering significances and defining and redefining ourselves. It is the most universal thing human beings do as in their secret hearts they work to achieve some positive effect in the world.

Over the next weeks and months what had been a slowly accumulating intention began to become resolve. On the day after Thanksgiving in 1965, when I was thirty-three years old, I started trying to write stories. Resolved that I would write every day, give it a lifetime of effort whether it worked or not, because success wasn't the point, I would get out of bed every morning before sunup, and type for an hour or so before going off to the ranch. I have learned to understand writing as useful precisely as that broken bit of woven matting and those bowls worn in the fundamental stone were useful to me. The stories are gestures, passing from one person to another, and they are part of a longer story that in this version begins with play and singing and mock warfare in a valley that is still naturally sacred and magically inhabited in my imagination—where, as Roethke said, "One learned of the eternal."

Redneck Secrets

BACK IN MY MORE SCATTERED days there was a time when I decided the solution to all life's miseries would begin with marrying a nurse. Cool hands and commiseration. She would be a second-generation Swedish girl who left the family farm in North Dakota to live a new life in Denver, her hair would be long and silvery blond, and she would smile every time she saw me and always be after me to get out of the house and go have a glass of beer with my buckaroo cronies.

Our faithfulness to each other would be legendary. We would live near Lolo, Montana, on the banks of the Bitterroot River where Lewis and Clark camped to rest on their way west, "Traveler's Rest," land that floods a little in the spring of the year, a small price to pay for such connection with mythology. Our garden would be intricately perfect on the sunny uphill side of our sixteen acres, with little wooden flume boxes to turn the irrigation water down one ditch or another.

We would own three horses, one a blue roan Appaloosa, and haul them around in our trailer to jackpot roping events on summer weekends. I wouldn't be much good on horseback, never was, but nobody would care. The saddle shed would be tacked to the side of our doublewide expando New Moon mobile home, and there would be a neat little lawn with a white picket fence about as high as your knee, and a boxer dog called Aces and Eights, with a great studded collar. There would be a .357 magnum pistol in the drawer of the bedside table, and on Friday night we would dance to the music of old-time fiddlers at some country tavern and in the fall we would go into the mountains for firewood and kill two or three elk for the freezer. There would be wild asparagus along the irrigation ditches and morels down under the cottonwoods by the river, and we would always be good.

And I would keep a journal, like Lewis and Clark, and spell bad, because in my heart I would want to be a mountain man—"We luved aft the movee in the bak seet agin tonite."

WE MUST NOT GAINSAY such Western dreams. They are not automatically idiot. There are, after all, good Rednecks and bad Rednecks. Those are categories.

So many people in the American West are hurt, and hurting. Bad Rednecks originate out of hurt and a sense of having been discarded and ignored by the Great World, which these days exists mostly on television, distant and most times dizzily out of focus out here in Redneck country.

Bad Rednecks lose faith and ride away into foolishness, striking back. The spastic utility of violence. The other night in a barroom, I saw one man turn to another who had been pestering him with drunken nonsense. "Son," he said, "you better calm yourself, because if you don't, things are going to get real Western here for a minute."

REAL WESTERN. Back in the late '40s when I was getting close to graduating from high school, they used to stage Saturday night prizefights down in the Veterans Auditorium. Not boxing matches but prizefights, a name that rings in the ear something like *cockfight*. One night the two main-event fighters, always heavyweights, were some hulking Indian and a white farmer from a little dairy-farm community.

The Indian, I recall, had the word "Mother" carved on his hairless chest. Not tattooed, but carved in the flesh with a blade, so the scar tissue spelled out the word in livid welts. The white farmer looked soft and his body was alabaster, pure white, except for his wrists and neck, which were dark, burned-in-the-fields red, burnished red. While they hammered at each other we hooted from the stands like gibbons, rooting for our favorites on strictly territorial and racial grounds, and in the end were all disappointed. The white farmer went down like thunder about three times, blood snorting from his nose in a delicate spray and decorating his whiteness like in, say, the movies. The Indian simply retreated to his corner and refused to go on. It didn't make any sense.

We screeched and stomped, but the Indian just stood there looking at the bleeding white man, and the white man cleared his head and looked at the Indian, and then they both shook their heads at each other, as if acknowledging some private news they had just then learned to share. They both climbed out of the ring and together made their way up the aisle. Walked away.

Real Western. Of course, in that short-lived partnership of the downtrodden, the Indian was probably doomed to a lifetime on the lower end of the seesaw. No dairy farms in a pastoral valley, nor morning milking and school boards for him. But that is not the essential point in this equation. There is a real spiritual equivalency between Redmen and Rednecks. How sad and ironic that they tend to hit at each other for lack of a real target, acting out some tired old scenario. Both, with some justice, feel used and cheated and disenfranchised. Both want to strike back, which may be just walking away, or the bad answer, bloody noses.

NOBODY IS CLAIMING certain Rednecks are gorgeous about their ways of resolving the pain of their frustrations. Some of them will indeed get drunk in honkytonks and raise hell and harass young men with long hair and golden earrings. These are the bad Rednecks.

Why bad? Because they are betraying themselves. Out-of-power groups keep fighting each other instead of what they really resent: power itself. A Redneck pounding a hippie in a dark barroom is embarrassing because we see the cowardice. What he wants to hit is a banker in broad daylight.

But things are looking up. Rednecks take drugs; hippies take jobs. And the hippie carpenters and the 250-pound, pigtailed lumberjacks preserve their essence. They are still isolated, outrageous, lonely, proud, and mean. Any one of them might yearn for a nurse, a doublewide, a blue roan Appaloosa, and a sense of place in a country that left him behind.

LIKE THE INDIAN and the buffalo on the old nickel, there are two sides to American faith. But in terms of Redneck currency, they conflict. On the one side there is individualism, which in its most radical mountain-man form becomes isolation and loneliness: the standard country-and-western lament. It will lead to dying alone in your motel room: whether gored, boozed, or smacked makes little difference. On the other side there are family and community, that pastoral society of good people inhabiting the good place on earth that William Bradford and Thomas Jefferson so loved to think about.

Last winter after the snowmobile races in Seeley Lake, I had come home to stand alongside my favorite bar rail and listen to my favorite skinny Redneck barmaid turn down propositions. Did I say *home*? Anyway, standing there and feeling at home, I realized that good Redneck bars are like good hippie bars: they are community centers, like churches and pubs in the old days, and drastically unlike our singles bars where every person is so radically his or her own.

My skinny barmaid friend looked up at one lumberjack

fellow, who was clomping around in his White logger boots
and smiling his most winsome. She said, "You're just one of
those boys with a sink full of dishes. You ain't looking for
nothing but someone dumb enough to come and wash your
dishes. You go home and play your radio."

A sink full of dirty dishes. And laundry. There are aspects of living alone that can be defined as going out to the
JCPenney store and buying $33 worth of new shorts and
socks and T-shirts because everything you own is stacked
up raunchy and stinking on the far side of the bed. And
going out and buying paper plates at Kmart because you're
tired of eating your meals crouched over the kitchen sink.
You finally learn about dirty dishes. They stay dirty. And
those girls, like my skinny friend, have learned a thing or
two. There are genuine offers of solace and companionship,
and there are dirty dishes and nursing. And then a trailer
house, and three babies in three years, diapers, and he's
gone to Alaska for the big money. So back to barmaiding,
this time with kids to support, baby-sitters.

Go home and play your radio.

THERE IS, OF COURSE, another Montana. Consider these
remarks from the journals of James and Granville Stewart,
1862:

> JANUARY 1, 1862. Snowed in the forenoon. Very
> cold in the afternoon. Raw east wind. Everybody
> went to grand ball given by John Grant at Grants-
> ville and a severe blizzard blew up and raged all
> night. We danced all night, no outside storm could
> dampen the festivities.
>
> JANUARY 2. Still blowing a gale this morning. Forty
> below zero and the air is filled with driving, drifting
> snow. After breakfast we laid down on the floor of

the several rooms, on buffalo robes that Johnny furnished, all dressed as we were and slept until about two-o'clock in the afternoon, when we arose, ate a fine dinner, then resumed dancing which we kept up with unabated pleasure . . . danced until sunrise.

JANUARY 3. The blizzard ceased about daylight, but it was very cold with about fourteen inches of snow badly drifted in places and the ground bare in spots. We estimated the cold at about thirty-five below, but fortunately there was but little wind. After breakfast all the visitors left for home, men, women, and children, all on horseback. Everyone got home without frost bites.

Sounds pretty good. But Granville Stewart got his. In the great and deadly winter of 1886–1887, before they learned the need of stacking hay for winter, when more than one million head of cattle ran the Montana ranges, he lost two-thirds of his cow herd. Carcasses piled in the coulees and fence corners come springtime, flowers growing up between the ribs of dead longhorn cattle, and the mild breezes reeking with decay. A one-time partner of Stewart's, Conrad Kohrs, salvaged 3,000 head out of 35,000. Reports vary, but you get the sense of it.

Over across the Continental Divide to where the plains begin on the east side of the Crazy Mountains, in the Two Dot country, on bright mornings you can gaze across the enormous swale of the Musselshell, north and east to the Snowy Mountains, fifty miles distant and distinct and clear in the air as the one mountain bluebell you picked when you came out from breakfast.

But we are not talking spring, we are talking winter and haystacks. A man we know, let's call him Davis Patten, is feeding cattle. It's February, and the snow is drifting three feet deep along the fence lines, and the wind is carrying the chill factor down to about thirty below. Davis Patten is pulling his feed sled with a team of yellow Belgian geldings. For this job, it's either horses or a track-layer, like a Caterpillar D-6. The Belgians are cheaper and easier to start.

Davis kicks the last remnant of meadow hay, still greenish and smelling of dry summer, off the sled to the trailing cattle. It's three o'clock in the afternoon and already the day is settling toward dark. Sled runners creak on the frozen snow. The gray light is murky in the wind, as though inhabited, but no birds are flying anywhere. Davis Patten is sweating under his insulated coveralls, but his beard is frozen around his mouth. He heads the team toward the barns, over under the cottonwood by the creek. Light from the kitchen windows shows through the bare limbs. After he has fed the team a bait of oats, then Davis and his wife Loretta will drink coffee laced with bourbon.

Later they watch television, people laughing and joking in bright Sony color. In his bones Davis recognizes, as most of us do, that the principal supporting business of television is lies, truths that are twisted about a quarter turn. Truths that were never truths. Davis drifts off to sleep in his Barca-Lounger. He will wake to the white noise from a gray screen.

It is important to have a sense of all this. There are many other lives, this is just one, but none are the lives we imagine when we think of running away to Territory.

Tomorrow Davis Patten will begin his day chopping ice along the creek with a splitting maul. Stock water, a daily chore. Another day with ice in his beard, sustained by memories of making slow love to Loretta under down comforters in their cold bedroom. Love, and then quickfooting it to the bathroom on the cold floors, a steaming shower. Memories of a bed that reeks a little of child making.

The rewards of the life, it is said, are spiritual, and often they are. Just standing on land you own, where you can dig any sort of hole you like, can be considered a spiritual reward, a reason for not selling out and hitting the Bahamas. But on his winter afternoons Davis Patten remembers another life. For ten years, after he broke away from Montana to the Marines, Davis hung out at the dragster tracks in the San Joaquin Valley, rebuilding engines for great, roaring, ass-busting machines. These days he sees their stripped red-and-white dragchutes flowering only on Sunday afternoons. The *Wide World of Sports*. Lost horizons. The intricate precision of cam shaft adjustments.

In the meantime, another load of hay.

UP IN TOWNS ALONG THE HIGHLINE, Browning and Harlem and Malta, people are continually dying from another kind of possibility. Another shot of Beam on the rocks and Annie Greensprings out back after the bars are closed. In Montana they used to erect little crosses along the highways wherever a fatality occurred. A while back, outside Browning, they got a dandy. Eleven deaths in a single car accident. *Guinness Book of World Records*. Verities. The highway department has given up the practice of erecting crosses: too many of them are dedicated to the disenfranchised.

Out south of Billings the great coal fields are being strip-mined. Possibilities. The history of Montana and the West, from the fur trade to tomorrow, is a history of colonialism, both material and cultural. Is it any wonder we are so deeply xenophobic and regard anything east of us as suspect? The money and the power always came from the East, took what it wanted, and left us, white or Indian, with our traditions dismantled and our territory filled with holes in the ground. Ever been to Butte? About half the old town was sucked into a vast open-pit mine.

Verities. The lasting thing we have learned here, if we

ever learn, is to resist the beguilements of power and money. Hang on to your land. There won't be any more. Be superstitious as a Borneo tribesman. Do not let them photograph our shy, bare-breasted beauties as they wash clothes along the stream bank. Do not let them steal your soul away in pictures, because they will if they get a chance, just as Beadle's Nickel-Dime Library westerns and Gene Autry B-movies gnawed at the soul of this country where we all live. Verities have to be earned, and they take time in the earning—time spent gazing out over your personal wind-glazed fields of snow. Once earned, they inhabit you in complex ways you cannot name, and they cannot be given away. They can only be transmogrified—transformed into something surreal or fantastic, unreal. And ours have been, and always for the same reason: primarily the titillation of those who used to be Easterners, who are everywhere now.

These are common sentiments here in the mountain West. In 1923 Charlie Russell agreed to speak before the Great Falls Booster Club. After listening to six or seven booster speeches, he tore up his own talk and spoke. This is what he said:

> In my book a pioneer is a man who turned all the grass upside down, strung bob-wire over the dust that was left, poisoned the water and cut down the trees, killed the Indian who owned the land, and called it progress. If I had my way, the land here would be like God made it, and none of you sons of bitches would be here at all.

So what are we left with? There was a great dream about a just and stable society, which was to be America. And there was another great dream about wilderness individuals, mountain men we have called them, who would be the natural defenders of that society. But our society is hugely corrupt, rich and impossibly complex, and our great simple individuals can define nothing to defend, nothing to reap but the isolation implicit in their stance, nothing to gain for their strength but loneliness. The vast, sad, recurrent story that is so centrally American. Western Rednecks cherish secret remnants of those dreams and still try to live within them. No doubt a foolish enterprise.

But that's why, full of anger and a kind of releasing joy, they plunge their Snowcats around frozen lakes at ninety miles an hour, coming in for a whiskey stop with eyes glittering and icicles bright on their whiskers, and why on any summer day you can look into the sky over Missoula and see the hang-gliding daredevils circling higher than the mountains. That's why you see grown men climbing frozen waterfalls with pretty colored ropes.

And then there seems to be a shooting a week in the doublewide village. Spastic violence. You know, the husband wakes up from his drunk, lying on the kitchen floor with the light still burning, gets himself an Alka-Seltzer, stumbles into the living room, and there is Mother on the couch with half her side blown away. The 12-gauge is carefully placed back where it belongs on the rack over the breakfront. Can't tell what happened. Must have been an intruder.

Yeah, the crazy man inside us. Our friends wear Caterpillar D-9 caps when they've never pulled a friction in their lives, and Buck knives in little leather holsters on their belts, as if they might be called upon to pelt out a beaver at any moment. Or maybe just stab an empty beer can. Ah, wilderness, and suicidal nostalgia.

Which gets us to another kind of pioneer we see these days, people who come to the country with what seems to be an idea that connection with simplicities will save their lives. Which simplicities are those? The condescension implicit in the program is staggering. If you want to feel you are being taken lightly, try sitting around while someone tells you how he envies the simplicity of your life. What about Davis Patten? He says he is staying in Montana and calling it home. So am I.

Despite the old Huckleberry Finn–mountain man notion of striking out for the territory, I am going to hang on here, best I can, and nourish my own self. I know a lovely woman who lives up the road in a log house, on what is left of a hard-earned farmstead. I'm going to call and see if she's home. Maybe she'll smile and come have a glass of beer with me and my cronies.

Drinking and Driving

DEEP IN THE FAR HEART of my upbringing, a crew of us sixteen-year-old lads were driven crazy with ill-defined midsummer sadness by the damp, sour-smelling sweetness of nighttime alfalfa fields, an infinity of stars and moonglow, and no girlfriends whatsoever. Frogs croaked in the lonesome swamp.

Some miles away over Warner Range was the little ranch and lumbermill town of Lakeview, with its whorehouse district. And I had use of my father's 1949 Buick. So, another summer drive. The cathouses, out beyond the rodeo grounds, were clustered in an area called Hollywood, which seemed right. Singing cowboys were part of everything gone wrong.

We would sink our lives in cheap whiskey and the ardor of sad, expensive women. In town, we circled past the picture show and out past Hollywood, watching the town boys and their town-boy business, and we chickened out on the whores and drank more beer, then drove on through the moonlight.

Toward morning we found ourselves looping higher and higher on a two-truck gravel road toward the summit of Mount Bidwell, right near the place where California and Nevada come together at the Oregon border. We topped out over a break called Fandango Pass.

The pass was named by wagon-train parties on the old Applegate cutoff to the gold country around Jacksonville. From that height they got their first glimpse of Oregon, and they camped on the summit and danced themselves some fandangos, whatever the step might be.

And we, in our ranch-boy style, did some dancing of our own. Who knows how it started, but with linked arms and hands we stumbled and skipped through the last shards of night and into the sunrise. Still drunk, I fell and bloodied my hands and stood breathing deep of the morning air and sucking at my own salty blood, shivering and pissing and watching the stunted fir and meadow aspen around me come luminous with light, and I knew our night of traveling had brought me to this happiness that would never bear talking about. No more nameless sorrow, not with these comrades, and we all knew it and remained silent.

Seventeen. I was safe forever, and I could see seventy miles out across the beauty of country where I would always live with these friends, all of it glowing with morning.

WE LEARN IT EARLY IN THE WEST, drinking and driving, chasing away from the ticking stillness of home toward some dim aura glowing over the horizon, call it possibility or excitement. Henry James once said there are two mental states, excitement and lack of excitement, and that unfortunately excitement was more interesting than lack of excitement. Travel the highways in Montana, and you will see little white crosses along the dangerous curves, marking places where travelers have died, many of them drunk, and most of them searching and unable to name what it was they were missing at home. It's like a sport: you learn techniques.

For instance, there are three ways to go: alone, with cronies of either sex, or with someone you cherish beyond all others at that particular moment. We'll call that one love and save it for last.

Although each of these modes can get tricky, alone is the most delicate to manage. Alone can lead to loneliness, and self-pity, and paranoia, and things like that—the trip can break down into dark questing after dubious companionship.

The advantage of going it alone lies, of course, in spontaneity and freedom. You don't have to consult anybody but your inclinations. You touch that warm car, and you climb in for a moment and roll down the window, just to see what it would be like.

And then, it's magic—you're rolling, you're gone, and you're riding. Shit fire, you think, they don't need me, not today. I'm sick. This is sick leave. You know it's true. You've been sick, and this day of freedom will cure your great illness. Adios.

Say it is spring, as in *to rise or leap suddenly and swiftly,* the most dangerous and frothy season, sap rising and the wild geese honking as they fly off toward the north. "Ensnared with flowers, I fall on grass." Andrew Marvell.

It might be the first day of everything, in which we rediscover a foreverland of freedom and beauty before the invention of guilt. A day when the beasts will all lie down with one another. Hummingbirds in the purple lilac.

What we are talking about is the first day of high and classical spring here in the temperate zones, one of those pure and artless mornings somewhere toward the latter part of May or early June in the countries where I have lived, when the cottonwood leaves have sprung from the bud and stand young and pale and green against the faint, elegant cleanliness of the sky. We are talking about walking outside into such a morning and breathing deeply.

Where I like to head out of Missoula is upstream along the Blackfoot River, the asphalt weaving and dipping and the morning light lime-colored through the new leaves on the aspen, with some fine, thin, fragile music cutting out from the tape deck, perhaps Vivaldi concerti played on the cello. Such music is important in the early day. It leaves a taste as clean as the air across the mountain pastures, and it doesn't encourage you to think. Later, there will be plenty of thinking.

But early on all I need is the music, and the motion of going, and some restraint. It always seems like a good idea, those mornings up along the Blackfoot, to stop at Trixie's Antler Inn just as the doors are being unlocked. One drink for the road and some banter with the hippie girl tending bar.

But wrong.

After the first hesitation, more stopping at other such establishments is inevitable. And quite enjoyable, one after another. The Wheel Inn on the near outskirts of Lincoln, Bowmans Corner over south of Augusta, with the front of the Rockies rearing on the western skyline like purity personified.

Soon that fine blue bowl of heaven and your exquisite freedom are forgotten, and you are talking to strangers and to yourself. No more Vivaldi. It's only noon, and you are playing Hank Williams tapes and singing along, wondering if you could have made it in the country-music business. By now you are a long and dangerous way from home and somewhat disoriented. The bartenders are studying you like a serious problem.

You have drifted into another mythology, called lonesome traveling and lost highways, a place where you really don't want to be on such a fine spring day. Once, it seemed like pure release to learn that you could vote with your feet, that you could just walk away like a movie star. Or, better yet, load your gear in some old beater pickup truck and drive. Half an hour, the vainglorious saying went, and I can have everything on rubber. Half an hour, and I'll be rolling. You just watch, little darling.

For some of us, the consequences of such escape tended to involve sitting alone with a pint bottle of whiskey in some ancient motel room where the television doesn't work. The concept was grand and theatrical, but doing it, getting

away, was oftentimes an emotional rat's nest of rootless-
ness. Country music, all that worn-out drifter syncopation,
turned out to be another lie, a terrific sport but a real thin
way of life.

SO, SOME RULES FOR GOING ALONE: forget destina-
tions; go where you will, always planning to stay overnight.
Stop at historical markers, and mull over the ironies of destiny as you drive on. By now you are listening to bluegrass,
maybe a tape from a Seldom Seen concert. And you are experiencing no despair.

Think of elk in the draws, buffalo on the plains, and the
complex precision of predator-prey relationships. Be interesting, and love your own company. There is no need to get
drunk and kill somebody on the road. Quite soon enough it
will be twilight, and you can stop in some little town, check
in at one of the two motels along the river, amble down to
the tavern, and make some new friends. Such a pretty life.

TRAVELING WITH CRONIES is another matter. Some obvious organizational efforts are implicit. There stands your
beloved car, warm in the sun. You touch a fender and turn
away and backtrack toward your telephone, which magically starts ringing. Others have the same idea. My rig, your
ice chest, bring money, we're traveling.

But the real logistical niceties lie in the chemistry of com-
patibility. Not just every good friend is a fit companion for
the heedless expeditions of a summer drive. Each stop and
turnoff must seem the result of consultation with mutual
inclination. Nothing spoils traveling more quickly than
endless debate, or any debate at all. Trust the driver. Everybody knows what we're looking for. Take us there.

Which is where? Looking for what? Call it ineffable—
that which cannot be expressed or described and is not to be

spoken of. Traveling with cronies can't be heedless without unspoken agreement.

Back when we were young and idiot, we would head up to The Stockman's in Arlee, hit the Buffalo Park in Ravalli, move on to the 44 Bar north of St. Ignatius, and then make the Charlo turn to Tiny's. From there whim led the way until we ended up in the Eastgate Lounge in Missoula around midnight. The circuit was called The Inner Circle.

SAY THE AFTERNOON SKY is streaked white, and spring winds drive storm clouds over the peaks of Montana's Mission Mountains. This is the Flathead Valley, and the town is Charlo, and though it may seem impersonal now, it need not be. If you are in any way sensible, your next move should be simple and clear and rewarding. You and your companions will clump down the stairs and into Tiny's Tavern. The place used to be called Tiny's Blind Pig, *blind pig* being prohibition code for tavern. The old name, for those of us who stopped by when we were passing through, implied a connection with the romance we were seeking— an outlaw dream of prohibition, dusty black automobiles just in from a rum-run to Canada, blond gum-snapping molls. As newcomers we ached to be a part of Montana— and here it was, the real goddamned item.

One night my brother was shooting pool at Tiny's with a wiry old man, an electrician by trade as I recall. During a lull in the bar talk I heard something that stood the hair on the back of my neck. "Son of a bitch," my brother said, "I wouldn't have to cheat to beat you."

Oh, pray for us, Lord. Outlanders in a bar filled with local ranchers and their brawny sons celebrating another victory for the best eight-man football team in the history of Montana. Do not let them beat on us—at least, not on me. Take my brother.

The rancher next to me, about a foot taller than I will ever be, looked sideways and grinned. "Don't know about you," he said, "but I ain't going over there. Them old black eyes take about three weeks to heal." By the time I had bought him and me a drink, my brother and the electrician were finishing their game without any further hint of warfare.

Well, I thought, got myself home again. Home is a notion such backcountry taverns seem to radiate—at least if they're places that long-time patrons and their barkeep hosts have imprinted with the wear and damage of their personalities. Tiny's was shaped as much as anything by the old man who owned it when I first went there—ancient and hurting, hobbling around on crutches, a former police chief from Miami, Florida, with a huge collection of memorabilia in glass cases around the bar—over 5,000 different kinds of beer bottles, intimate snapshots of Hitler taken in the 1930s, fine obsidian arrowheads, gem-quality Kennedy half-dollars. Tiny is dead now, and they've changed the sign over the doorway. But his collections are still in place.

Homes and love, if they are to exist as more than fond children of the imagination, most often take us by surprise on back roads. On my way to Missoula almost every day I pass the old Milltown Union Bar, where Dick Hugo used to do his main drinking in the days when he was serious about it. Above the doorway white heads of mountain goat and bighorn sheep, sealed in Plexiglas bubbles, contemplate those who enter. As Hugo said in a poem about the Milltown, "You were nothing going in, and now you kiss your hand." In another poem, about another barroom, Hugo named the sense of recognition and homecoming I expect upon going into one of the taverns I love. His poem begins, "Home. Home. I knew it entering."

INDEED, WHAT ARE WE LOOKING FOR? In July of 1969 I came to Montana to stay, bearing a new Master of Fine Arts degree from the flooding heartland of Iowa. I had just finished up as a thirty-five-year-old, in-off-the-ranch graduate student in the Iowa Writers' Workshop, and I had lucked into a teaching job at the University of Montana. I was running to native cover in the West; I was a certified writer, and this was the beginning of my real life at last.

During that summer in Iowa City—drinking too much, in love with theories about heedlessness and possibility—I was trying to figure out how to inhabit my daydream. We lived in an old stone-walled house with a flooded basement out by the Coralville reservoir, listening to cockroaches run on the nighttime linoleum and imagining Montana, where we would find a home.

Every morning the corn in the fields across the road looked to have grown six inches, every afternoon the skies turned green with tornado-warning storms, and every night lightning ran magnificent and terrible from the horizons. My wife said they ought to build a dike around the whole damned state of Iowa and turn it into a catfish preserve. The U-Haul trailer was loaded. After a last party we were history in the Midwest, gone to Montana, where we were going to glow in the dark.

The real West started at the long symbolic interstate bridge over that mainline to so many ultimately heartbreaking American versions of heaven, the Missouri River. Out in the middle of South Dakota I felt myself released into significance. It was clear I was aiming my life in the correct direction. We were headed for a town studded with abandoned tepee burners.

But more so—as we drove I imagined Lewis and Clark and Catlin and Bodmer and even Audubon up to Fort Union on the last voyage of his life in 1843, along with every wagon train, oxcart, cattle drive, and trainload of honyockers, all in pursuit of that absolute good luck that is some breathing time in a commodious place where the best that can be is right now. In the picture book of my imagination I was seeing a Montana composed of major postcards. The great river sliding by under the bridge was rich with water from the Sun River drainage, where elk and grizzly were rumored to be on the increase.

Engrossed in fantasies of traveling upriver into untouched territory, I was trying to see the world fresh, as others had seen it. On April 22, 1805, near what is now the little city of Williston in North Dakota, Meriwether Lewis wrote:

> . . . immense herds of buffalo, elk, deer, and antelopes feeding in one common and boundless pasture. We saw a large number of beaver feeding on the bark of trees along the verge of the river, several of which we shot. Found them large and fat.

By 1832, at the confluence of the Missouri and the Yellowstone, the painter George Catlin was already tasting ashes while trying to envision a future—just as I was trying to imagine what had been seen. Catlin wrote:

> . . . the native Indian in his classic attire, galloping his wild horse, with sinewy bow, and shield and lance, amid the fleeting herds of elks and buffaloes. What a beautiful and thrilling specimen for America to preserve and hold up to the view of her refined citizens and the world, in future ages! A *nation's park,* containing man and beast, in all the wild and freshness of their nature's beauty!

Think of Audubon responding eleven years later, on May 17, 1843, in that same upriver country around Fort Union:

> Ah! Mr. Catlin, I am now sorry to see and to read
> your accounts of the Indians you saw—how very
> different they must have been from any that I have
> seen!

On July 21, Audubon writes:

> What a terrible destruction of life, as it were for
> nothing, or next to it, as the tongues only were
> brought in, and the flesh of these fine animals were
> left to beasts and birds of prey, or to rot on the spots
> where they fell. The prairies were literally covered
> with the skulls of victims.

On August 5 Audubon finishes the thought:

> But this cannot last; even now there is a perceptible
> difference in the size of the herds, and before many
> years the Buffalo, like the Great Auk, will have dis-
> appeared; surely this should not be permitted.

In our summer of 1969 we poked along the edge where
the Badlands break so suddenly from the sunbaked prairies,
imagining the faraway drumming of hooves, Catlin's warriors on their decorated horses coming after us from somewhere out of dream. Not so far south lay Wounded Knee.

We studied the stone faces of our forefathers at Mount
Rushmore and didn't see a damned thing because by that
time in the afternoon we were blinded by so much irony on
a single day. We retired for the night to a motel somewhere
south of the Devil's Postpile in Wyoming. I was seeing
freshly, but not always what I hoped to see. The distances
were terrifying.

By the time we reached Missoula, I had disassociated
my sensibilities with whiskey, which gave me the courage to
march up the concrete steps to Richard Hugo's house, only
a block from the Clark Fork River, where the Village Inn

Motel sits these days. I rapped on his door. He studied me a moment after I introduced myself. "You're very drunk," he said.

Well hell, I thought, now you've done it.

"Wait a minute," Hugo said. "I'll join you."

Home, I thought, childlike with relief. This was the new country I had been yearning for, inhabited by this man who smiled and seemed to think I should be whatever I could manage.

I WAS LUCKY TO KNOW DICK HUGO, and his collected poems, *Making Sure It Goes On,* heads my list of good books written about the part of the world where I live. Dick loved to drive Montana, his trips imaginative explorations into other lives as a way toward focusing on his own complexities. He made the game of seeing into art, and his poetry and life form a story that lies rock-bottom in my understanding of what art is for.

Once we drove over to fish the Jefferson River on a summer day when we were both hungover to the point of insipid visionary craziness. We didn't catch any fish, and I came home numb, simply spooked, but Dick saw some things and wrote a poem:

Silver Star

This is the final resting place of engines,
farm equipment and that rare, never more
than occasional man. Population:
17. Altitude unknown. For no
good reason you can guess, the woman
in the local store is kind. Old steam trains
have been rusting here so long, you feel

the urge to oil them, to lay new track, to start
the west again. The Jefferson
drifts by in no great hurry on its way
to wed the Madison, to be a tributary
to the ultimately dirty brown Missouri.
This town supports your need to run alone.

What if you'd lived here young, gone full of fear
to that stark brick school, the cruel teacher
supported by your guardian? Think well
of the day you ran away to Whitehall.
Think evil of the cop who found you starving
and returned you, siren open, to the house
you cannot find today. The answer comes back wrong.
There was no house. They never heard your name.

When you leave, leave in a flashy car
and wave goodbye. You are a stranger
every day. Let the engines and the farm
equipment die, and know that rivers
end and never end, lose and never lose
their famous names. What if your first girl
ended certain she was animal, barking
at the aides and licking floors? You know
you have no answers. The empty school
burns red in heavy snow.

Each time I read "Silver Star" I rediscover a story about
homes, and the courage to acknowledge such a need, a story
about Dick and his continual refinding of his own life, and
an instruction about storytelling as the art of constructing
road maps, ways home to that ultimate shelter which is the
coherent self. Montana is a landscape reeking with such
conjunction and resonance. They fill the silence.

Not long ago, on a bright spring morning, I stood on the cliffs of the Ulm Pishkun where the Blackfeet drove dusty hundreds of bison to fall and die. Gazing east I could dimly see the great Anaconda Company smokestack there on the banks of the Missouri like a finger pointing to heaven above the old saloon-town city of Great Falls where Charlie Russell painted and traded his pictures for whiskey—only a little upstream from the place where Meriwether Lewis wrote, having just finished an attempt at describing his first sight of the falls:

> After writing this imperfect description, I again viewed the falls, and was so much disgusted with the imperfect idea it conveyed of the scene, that I determined to draw my pen across it and begin again; but then reflected that I could not perhaps succeed better. . . .

After so many months of precise notation, all in the service of Thomas Jefferson's notion of the West as useful, in one of the most revealing passages written about the American West, Lewis seems to be saying: *But this, this otherness is beyond the capture of my words, this cannot be useful, this is dream.* The dam-builders, of course, did not see it his way.

Behind me loomed the fortress of the rock-sided butte Charlie Russell painted as a backdrop to so much history, with the Rockies off beyond on the western horizon, snowy and gleaming in the morning sun. This listing could go on, but I was alone and almost frightened by so many conjunctions visible at once, and so many others right down the road: the Gates of the Mountains and Last Chance Gulch and even make-believe—Boone Caudill and Teal Eye and Dick Summers over west on the banks of the Teton River, where it cuts through the landscapes of *The Big Sky*—

history evident all around and the imaginings of artists and storytellers intertwined. Charlie Russell and Bud Guthrie and Dick Hugo and Meriwether Lewis created metaphoric territory as real as any other Montana in the eye of my imagination.

We all play at transporting ourselves new into new country, seeing freshly, reorienting ourselves and our schemes within the complexities of the world. It is a powerful connection to history, and the grand use we make of storytelling as we incessantly attempt to recognize that which is sacred and the point of things.

WHICH BRINGS US to our most complex option, traveling with lovers. In Missoula, in the heart of winter, if you are me, you talk in a placating way to the woman you love. It is about three days after you forgot another country custom, The Valentine Party. You suggest ways of redeeming yourself. You talk to friends. An expedition forms.

This paragon of a woman owns an aging four-wheel-drive Chevrolet pickup, three-quarter-ton, and she and I and her twin boys set off in that vehicle. Only praying a little bit. Good rubber, but a clanking U-joint. The friends—a southern California surfer hooked on snow skiing of all varieties, and a lady of his acquaintance—set off in that lady's vintage Volvo. We also pray for them. The Volvo wanders in its steering, in a somewhat experimental way. But no need for real fear. These are Montana highways.

Out of Missoula we caravan south through the Bitterroot Valley, where—before the subdivisions—Tom Jefferson could have seen his vision of pastoral American happiness realized. The Volvo wanders, the U-joint clanks, and we are happy. We wind up over Lost Trail Pass, where Lewis and Clark experienced such desperate vertigo in the wilderness on their way west. At the summit we turn east, toward the Big Hole Basin and a town named Wisdom. At 6,000 feet, the altitude in the Big Hole is too much for deciduous trees. The only color is the willow along the creeks, the red of dried blood.

We pass along the Big Hole Battlefield, where Joseph and Looking Glass and the Nez Percés suffered ambush by Federal troops under General Oliver Otis Howard on the morning of August 11, 1877. Casualties: Army, 29 killed, 40 wounded; Nez Percé, by Army body count, 89 dead, most of them women and children. We are traveling through the rich history of America.

Winter has come down on this country like a hammer, but the defroster is working perfectly and there is a bar in Wisdom with dozens of stuffed birds and animals on display around the walls. The place is crowded with weekend snowmobile fans in their bright insulated nylon coveralls. There is a stuffed quail on a stand with its head torn off. All that's left is just a little wire sticking out of its neck. What fun that night must have been.

The bar is fine. No one cares when we bring in our own cheeses and stoneground wheat crackers. We slice on the bar top, scatter crumbs. The bartender cleans up our mess. Smiles. The kids play the pinball machine all they want. We have hot drinks. So we are slightly tipsy, not to say on the verge of drunk, when we line out south toward Jackson. This is the deep countryside of Montana, and no one cares. The Volvo doesn't wander as erratically. The U-joint has made peace with itself. Which is something country people know about mechanical devices. They oftentimes heal. At least for a little while.

The Big Hole is called the "Land of 10,000 Haystacks." Nearby, a country man is feeding his cattle. Pitching hay with ice in his mustache. He has been doing it every day for two months. He has a month to go. Feeding cattle never was any fun. We do not think about such matters.

Beyond Polaris we head up a canyon between five-foot banks of snow and we are arrived. Elkhorn Hot Springs. Right away, we like it. Snowshoeing and cross-country in all directions, and for our surfer friend, a dandy little down-hill area only about three miles away. We have a cabin with a fireplace that works fine after the wood dries out. Up in the lodge they are serving family-style dinners. And cheap. You know—roast beef and meat loaf and real mashed potatoes and creamed corn and pickled beets. And on and on. Maybe this is the moment to break out the bottle of rum.

Eventually we wander down to the hot baths, the indoor sauna pools and the outdoor pool, and the snow falling into our mouths. Snowball fights in the water. Rowdiness. Young boys in swimming suits created from cutoff Levis. And the next day, sweet red wine in the snow and white chilled wine in the evening, and the ache from all the skiing melting out of our knees into the hot water.

But electricity is in fact the way nature behaves. Nothing lasts. That was winters ago. My surfer friend went off hunting the last good wave. He wrote from Australia, extolling the virtues of the unexamined life. The Volvo is dead; the U-joint is fixed. Desire and the pursuit of the whole is called love.

Overthrust Dreams: 1981

SEE THEM COMING, headlights out of the dust over the Wyoming desert north of Evanston. These are the rough-necks, oil-field hands, latter-day warriors in this combat zone of American energy solutions. They are coming off shift and burning with real money and fine innocent hubris. Later tonight in the barrooms they will grin and look you in the eye and call themselves cannon fodder. But you know, goddamnit, that they don't mean it. They are boomers, and they are spinning through the urgent main adventure of their manhood, and they love these days without shame.

These broken-fingered youngsters are the princes of our latest disorder. And this is Christmastime, our most hopeful season. They stomp the streets of Evanston in their moon boots, felt-lined Sorels like the ones you can buy from the L. L. Bean catalogue, their uniform a pair of damp cover-alls sheened and splattered with drilling mud. They tip their yellow hard hats to the ladies while they figure some way to feed themselves in a town without franchise foods, and they get revved up for another night of shooting pool in some joint like the Pink Pony, or for courting the Mormon girls who flock up the sixty miles from Ogden to the Whirl Inn Disco Bar. Roughnecks. They like the name.

ME AND THE HONORABLE SCHOOLBOY, my friend and guide in that land, were picking up some fried chicken breasts from the deli in the Evanston IGA store. We were going to carry our food a couple of blocks to the Laundro-mat and eat there in the bright warmth amid odors of de-tergent and bleach, sharing space with the young oil-patch wives and their knots of beggar children. A clean, well-lighted place, a haven. *Got those all-night Laundromat blues, washed everything but my shoes.* Christmastime in Evanston.

Out on the main drag, 90 percent of the vehicles were new-model 4×4s, tape decks squalling some symbolic version of "Sympathy for the Devil," most of them burning diesel pumped from tanks alongside the great Caterpillar and White engines that power the drilling rigs. In a stricter, less dynamic world, that would be called theft. Here in the heartland of our heedlessness it is called small potatoes.

SO MANY AMERICAN DREAMS are woven, like strands in a rope, from two notions: radical freedom and pastoral communalism. The cold boomtown distances in the West have always been traveled and inhabited by those who want both in an improbably happy package containing money and something else, something more complex, something that stays secret, sensed rather than known, always there to be yearned toward.

The Young Roughneck, a crony of the Honorable Schoolboy, was talking about Christmas. About tree decorating and the strings of popcorn they used to drape on the boughs back when he was a hired-hand poorboy in the wholesome dairy country of Wisconsin. Before he got wise and went chasing over to Madison for the strobe-light concerts and rebellion in the parking lots, the small-time dope peddling and a couple counts of car theft before he was voting age.

But all that was behind him now. The Young Roughneck was talking household gifts, like maybe a little battery-powered coffee-bean grinder of modernistic NASA-inspired design. On the shopping-center hippie fringes of Salt Lake City he had discovered the pleasures of fresh-ground Viennese Blend. So no more Instant Folgers for this child. Not after Xmas.

"Just going to buy me that little whirring son of a bitch," he said. "Cash money." He looked across the breakfast table and grinned. A roll of folding money like the one he dug out of his pocket equals a start toward shareholding in America. No more teacher's dirty looks.

Outdoors, the morning was bright and clean bluebird, four inches of glittering old snow and zero degrees. We were thirty miles north of Evanston, in the gut of the drilling country, where the Young Roughneck and the Honorable Schoolboy and some others had spent the previous summer camped on BLM land while they worked the towers—squatters alongside a spring some rancher dug out and piped into troughs for his livestock in the old days, before Amoco and Chevron started deep drilling in a serious way.

Shaking the chill and some hungover nerves, we were sipping coffee laced with Crown Royal and sitting jammed into the jacked-up pickup camper where the Young Roughneck resided full-time with his wife, the Cornflower Bride, a pretty girl of nineteen with a blue cornflower tattooed onto her right breast, and their year-old son, the Oilfield Urchin, a bright-eyed winsome lad. The seating was a little cramped, but the hospitality was generous, and we were plenty warm. Could have been more desperate.

Down the road a mile or so, in what they called Ragtown, where drifting roughnecks had lived all last summer in tents or less, packing water from a rancher's spring and cooking over open fires when they came off shift, there was still one stalwart roughneck living in his automobile, a late-model General Motors product. The exact make was hard to fix, since it was covered over with old blankets and tarps for insulation. The only heat in there was a two-burner Coleman stove. Light up and risk asphyxiation. Or stay tough and freeze a trifle.

The idea was: live close to the work and the time-and-a-half for overtime, which could often amount to sixty hours and a thousand dollars a week even for the mildly skilled.

"Yeap," the Young Roughneck said. "Executive wages."

Well, maybe not quite, but freedom. The previous summer one of the boomers from Ragtown had run his big-tired diesel Ford pickup down to Ogden and hauled back about three thousand dollars worth of motel furniture from a wholesale outlet, everything but a TV, and set up housekeeping in the sagebrush around a fire ring. He lived there like a crowned king of the imagination until October, when the rains commenced. He left the stuff sitting and headed back to winter in Texas. Radical freedom, a deer rifle you feel no need to fire, a fly rod from Orvis, and a $600 tape deck and transoceanic radio: everything on rubber, and open roads.

The Young Roughneck and family said they were staying until spring, according to the latest plans, and then they were taking a vacation tour of national parks in their pickup camper. For Christmas they were going to go down to Salt Lake City and rent the best motel room in town for two or three days and buy presents and set up a tree. The Oilfield Urchin was going to have himself a traditional time, tearing up bright tissue-paper wrappings. And the first package they would open was going to be the Polaroid camera.

An old sweet story. Our central privilege as Americans has always been our luck—the spectacular heritage of the great good places in which we live. Since the days of the Puritans, we have been defoliating that heritage, mining it in one sense or another, as if it were inexhaustible. As if there were no tomorrow.

~

That which is not useful is vicious
—COTTON MATHER

FOR MOST OF 350 YEARS, Americans have acted as if he were right, and not insane, as if the spaces amid which we reside, outside Evanston or anywhere else, were as alien as the moon.

And we still do, which accounts for the voices in Evanston. "Well, shit," you heard them say. "It's just the goddamned desert. They really aren't hurting nothing."

The local folks knew what they were losing. But they seemed unwilling to recognize how very expendable the homeland of their childhoods had become, how truly it was being sacrificed.

The rewards of petroleum figured large in imaginations around Evanston—airline tickets to romantic places and new hay balers for the ranchers, easy sex and pure, clean drugs and booze, and the dancing beguilements of rock-and-roll for the roughnecks. And they led people into wistful thinking. Maybe, just this one time—so the reasoning went—we can drill and grade this desert a little bit more to death, and then we will quit. Then we will be home, to live out our lives in harmony with the dictates of our secret hearts, at peace with the blossoming earth.

THE BOTTOM LINE around Evanston was beyond all sensible reckoning, too long for a lifetime of finger counting, something reasonable only to the make-believe computers: One Hundred Billion Dollars.

One hundred times a thousand million dollars. That is how much, in 1980, we in the United States spent importing foreign petroleum. That was one hellacious load of economic thrust, much of it aimed into boomtowns like Casper and Evanston and Gillette and Wamsutter in Wyoming, and in Rangely down in Colorado.

The Ryckman Creek oilfield north of Evanston had estimated reserves worth far more than $500 million at

1980 prices, and in the Whitney Canyon fields there was an estimated reserve of natural gas that was priced at over $800 million. Amoco predicted that the area's total reserves would amount to the energy equivalent of about one-quarter of the reserves in Prudhoe Bay, the Alaskan field producing almost 10 percent of the nation's oil.

Though reports vary widely, oil companies had spent at least $250 million in the Evanston area by 1981. This Wyoming cow town—four or five blocks of hardware stores and notions shops, a single theater, a half-dozen bars, neat houses under Chinese elms and lilac blooming in springtime, a string of motels out by the freeway off-ramp, and a population of 4,500 in the mid-1970s—this town had 4,000 transient newcomers already, and another 4,000 expected, along with 60 to 100 new drilling rigs. It's an old western story: the boomtown syndrome.

The litany of ills has always been much the same, whether we're talking about old-time cow towns like Caldwell, Kansas, or contemporary company towns like Colstrip, Montana; lumber towns like Mabel, Oregon, or military communities like Mohave, Arizona. In *Roughing It* Mark Twain talks about the town of Unionville in Nevada, where "We were stark mad with excitement—drunk with happiness—smothered under mountains of prospective wealth."

The beginning was always characterized by careless haste in the expectation of landing in the chips, quick profit for the skillful, and luck; city planning generally nonexistent or close to it; and residents willing to pay almost any price for whatever it was they wanted, from dentistry in the old days to cocaine in Evanston. The central theme has always been easy money, followed by large numbers of people, gambling, prostitution, sewage problems, and all the macho you could hope for—combining to make law enforcement nearly impossible, undermining respect for what have been called the "civilized virtues" of home: the arts, regular bathing, and literature.

And then the money runs out, and everybody leaves for somewhere else. The city fathers of Evanston were aware of all this. In the late 1970s they were shocked into a possible vision of the future by the drug-crazed, cathouse horror show in Rock Springs, 80 miles east on Interstate 80 and already deep into the energy boomtown syndrome. Not here, they said, and they did a reasonable job of holding that line. That's why there were no fast-food franchises in Evanston. Outsiders had an expensive time getting building permits.

But already raw sewage was being dumped into Bear River, which runs through the outskirts of town, and older, single-story houses cost nearly $100,000, with damned few on the market. Parking space for a mobile home cost $250 a month, without water and sewage connections, and the waiting list ran as long as your arm. Living in a motel room decorated with plants to make it feel like a home cost $1,000 a month. The Ramada Inn, when I was there, had no rooms and didn't expect to have any soon. Hundreds, including company men from the oil towers, got their mail General Delivery because all the post-office boxes had long since been allocated. The roads were torn up, the schools were jammed, property taxes had gone up beyond all reason, bar fights and family shoot-outs and all-around thievery were becoming commonplace: the old community was trying to hold on but was increasingly engulfed, at the same time growing richer and richer, some say sacrificed.

"They have strung us up," a hardened downtown Evanston businessman told me, "and take it or leave it, like it or maybe, they are skinning our hides. Right away they're going to start cutting steaks." At the time he was buying drinks for the house about every twenty minutes, paying for them with one fifty-dollar bill after another.

Outside the Young Roughneck's jacked-up camper, after one final pull straight from the Crown Royal bottle, we watched a seismic-survey helicopter lift from a hilltop over north toward the Chase tower, the drilling rig where my friends had worked until the previous week.

During deer season the previous fall some hunter had brought down one of the helicopters. One high-powered rifle shot to the guts, smoke and explosions and a modified crash landing. Late that summer a rancher from down on the hay-land flat beside the Bear River had driven up in midday and dropped a dead and reeking badger into the tank of fresh spring water that all the campers were using for drinking and cooking. The snowy Uinta Mountains down across the Utah border gleamed in the sunlight, and we were reminded that problem-solving tends to run toward direct action in places where the air is so clean.

My friends were not working because they'd got themselves fired for fighting on the rig. They'd been working a morning tower from midnight until eight, and one of the hands showed up drunk with four of his friends and started beating on the motor man. That led quickly to group loyalties and bloodshed. One fellow took a ball-peen hammer to the head, and it will be some time before he remembers his name.

But not to worry. The cops ran those boys out of town, and in this boomer world jobs are never a problem. At least not for long. Just start roaming around from rig to rig after the midnight shift change, and you will find some crew where a man showed up drunk or too stoned to function, or not at all, and they will be coming out of the hole with 10,000 feet of 5-inch pipe, getting ready to replace the triple-headed Howard Hughes drilling bit, and right away you will have a job. Downtime on these rigs costs about $1,000 an hour, so they like to keep them turning.

But the Honorable Schoolboy didn't want a job. Starting in June as a green hand, he'd learned to work every spot on the rig—"from the crown to the ground," as they say— and he'd saved up better than $10,000 by the winter. That was enough for a year in film school at UCLA, with some weeks in the summer for climbing in Yosemite.

The Young Roughneck, who had never finished his third year of high school, did not have those options, and things between them, on this score, were a little tricky. But what the hell, this is a world of come-and-go, and they both knew that the sons of stockbrokers and physicians don't look to spend the rest of their lives roughnecking on the towers. In winter there is a limit to the utility of romance.

They shook hands and looked away. Catch you later, in some other lifetime.

"He's got that girl," the Honorable Schoolboy said as we drove away. "Out here that's like a gift. Most of them just got the work, and that's a hard place to find your pride." Then he smiled at himself for having absorbed too much Hemingway. Men without women, and the complex attractiveness of combat zones.

When they asked me what I was doing in Evanston I would say anthropologist. Journalists and sociologists have a history of getting beat up here. It's a new roughneck sport—thumping on the pudgy creeps who come to study them as if they were a hill of ants.

When I told the woman down at the bar that I was an anthropologist, she looked as if she didn't believe me.

She was one of a tribe called Morning-Tower Widows; at least that's how I saw her at first glance. Married to men who work the morning tower, these women sleep out the days and drink away the evenings. This one was attractive in a lean and redheaded 37-year-old way, all her visible parts covered with freckles the size and color of pennies, and she was well into a red beer at 9:15 on a Saturday morning, wiping her lips with a napkin after each sip.

"God's truth," I told her. "Anthropology."

"If it gives them something," she said, "why not."

Turned out she was talking tattoos. People bouncing trailer court to trailer court can lose track of every blessed thing but themselves, and they start having multicolored pictures engraved on their skin. "Only thing they got," she said. "Keeps them company at night, while they are praying to themselves."

She was married to a helicopter pilot, and they lived sixty miles down the road in the Utah ski-resort town of Park City. "No more of these rat towns," she said, twisting her mouth as if the beer had gone sour. "We drink in them class bars, and we own the condo. So things are just fine. Them hippie girls got themselves to blame. Some gotta win and some gotta lose."

She looked dead into me with her dry, gray, redhead eyes and bought me a drink as she was walking out. So much for the romance of morning drinking, Morning-Tower Widows, and the anthropology of self-deception.

THE HONORABLE SCHOOLBOY and I headed to the Chase rig on the hill. Most of the leases around Evanston were held by Amoco and Chevron, but the actual drilling was done under contract by specialty firms such as Brinkerhoff and Chase and Parker. The Schoolboy was hoping to pick up his last paycheck, about $1,500 earned before the fighting broke out.

But right away we saw that the drilling pipe was stuck in a hole, and the Honorable Schoolboy got worried. They were fishing, as they call it on rigs, sending complex tools down the hole, to about 9,500 feet in this case, latching onto the pipe and trying to break it loose by a series of complex twistings and jerkings from whatever formation it's locked into. The basic idea in this kind of operation is to get the pipe up so the drill bit can be replaced. So far they'd had about 30 hours of downtime, at the infamous $1,000 an hour, and tempers were most likely running mean.

The deep holes, down to 15,000 feet in many wells, were tough propositions, hard to hold straight as the bits cut through the slanting ledges so far below. The rigs are enormous steel-girder structures towering 120 feet above the desert, and they work in a long, repetitive rhythm—at most 200 hours through the entire cycle. That's the best you'll ever get from one of those high-rental Hughes drill bits.

Most of the work takes place on what is called "the floor," a wide, enclosed platform some thirty feet off the ground, atop the substructure that houses the huge flower of blow-out protection valves designed to prevent the trememdous hydraulic pressures of the earth from blowing deadly H_2S gas into their faces. In case the valves don't work, there are gas masks. It's like war. In case of gas, the rule is: kill for a mask, if you must. Repent later.

All the work is dangerous on these small-scale factories in the wilderness. Enormous weight hangs above the floor on cables—the Kelly gear head that turns the drilling, the huge block and tackle used to lift the tons of drilling pipe from the hole while they are changing bits—and cables can break; everything can come down. The wrap of chain used to turn the pipe into its threads can fly loose from the hands of the chain man and take off your head. Or the derrick man, ninety-five feet above your head, can drop a Coca-Cola can just after he pops the top.

Going out to such work, shift to shift, breeds hardness, and contempt for those who give it up. The Tool Pusher on the Chase rig that morning didn't have much time for the Honorable Schoolboy. Class differences, if you will, matters of vocabulary. And he was pissed to be bothered with the trivialities of a boy seeking a paycheck.

And the paycheck, the $1,500, was not there. The Tool Pusher, an old Texas professional, exasperated by all these long-haired dropout newcomers, finally recalled that he had sent it back to the drilling company. "Shit," he said, grinning cold at the Honorable Schoolboy. "I got no time to baby-sit your money."

Comes with the territory. The money, which he would no doubt recover in time, didn't bother the Honoroable Schoolboy so much as this shitty way of leaving a line of work he had gone at with pride and determination. "That's Evanston," he said, and my mind heard the last line from *Chinatown.*

"Forget it, Jake."

THE BOEING 707 LIFTED from Salt Lake International into a bright morning. The flats below were covered with the undulations of a luminous ground fog that had burned at our eyes, and off west the snowy mountains of desert Utah and Nevada stood shattering-white and intricate against the sheltering endlessness of clean sky, each rockfall precisely defined by shadow. Bingham Canyon—the world's largest open-pit mine—was also lovely in its unnatural way, down there under the new snowfall, a vast spiral of earth sculpture, like the Tower of Babel turned upside down.

These occasional visions of our landscape produce another sort of bottom line. Those of us who live in the West, our better selves mirrored in a great and clean good place, must weigh that image against a long history of rootless boomtown extravagance that is equally our heritage.

The locals try to pretend their lives aren't changing; the boomers swagger through town with burning money in their pockets; and the professionals do their work and try to live somewhere else, maybe down in Park City, among the skiers.

And the sociologists and journalists, people like me, come to view the rush of vitality and rich-kid chaos as if it were theater, another episode in the Wild West Extravaganza. Out along the frozen-over meadows along Bear River north of Evanston I rode a creaking hay wagon with a man who had been born in the house where he lived. "The sons-a-bitches," he said. "I got some of their lease money, and I like it fine."

"But goddam," he said. "That was country I knew, each and every rise and fall of it, and now she is roads and derricks and a lost cause. The only pretty thing out there is those towers at night, lighted up like Christmas trees."

Grizzly

STARLIGHT IS BEGINNING to show off the lake water. In this mountaintop land we are absolutely isolated, except for the fire burning near the rocky shoreline, the flitterings of light touching at our bright tent. Occasionally a trout rises and splashes, and the rings undulate away on the perfect stained-glass stillness of the water.

Someone claims to have heard the distant crackling of branches, but this is wilderness and now the only sounds are the faint humming of the earth and the snapping of the pine-knot fire. Under the clean, smoky odor we rebuild the fire and finally drift to sleep. Then you feel a hand clutching at yours, and you come slowly awake into awareness that this is not a dream.

There is a snuffling sound outside the tent, and the grunting of some animal; it comes twice, and then the fabric is ripped away, and the vast dark animal is there in the faint glow of the fire, silent and intent as someone prepares to scream, and then there is the screaming, the quick scuffling movements, and the quiet after the screaming, which stopped so abruptly.

A FRIEND OF MINE, Mary Pat Mahoney, was killed by a grizzly in 1976, over in the Many Glaciers Campground of Glacier National Park, about a hundred and fifty yards from the Ranger Station. Contemplation of her death led me to that dream, a waking nightmare I learned to articulate at home in my bed the nights after she was dragged from her tent. It thinned any mountain-man resolve I might ever have possessed to spend a pleasant campfire evening in the vicinity.

Up here on this night, however, we are barricaded from whatever might be out there, and we have been speculating about loss of reverence for that which is majestic and legitimately awesome, and about the usefulness of all creatures, particularly the fearful usefulness of the great *ursus arctos horribilis,* the grizzly.

We have been talking habitat and viable populations, and carnivorous predator-prey relationships. And outside, a frog is eating the moon. That's an old Native American legend about a phenomenon we know as lunar eclipse.

We are in the midst of the best grizzly country left below the Canadian border, high up on the lookout tower atop Huckleberry Ridge, the peaks of Glacier National Park looming eastward in the silvery light, and we are talking sociobiology and primitive religion, primate social behavior, and the notion that reason springs from humility.

The full moon of this mid-July night is more than half gone behind the earth's shadows. We are talking confrontations and reasons for courting fear.

Our host on the mountain, Doug Peacock, when he is not out on the veranda cranking away at the eclipse with his old spring-wound 16mm Bolex movie camera, is sipping at our bottle of Glenlivet whisky and imitating the ways the grizzlies conduct themselves when interacting with their own kind and when facing down humans.

In his jam-packed 15-by-15-foot room atop the lookout tower, Peacock is standing tall on his toes and eyeing us like we are invaders of his most prime ripe berry patch, then dropping and hunching his back and growling and circling at us with a kind of quartering half-drunk and rough-handed playfulness.

"Yeah, for damned sure," he says, and his eyes are gleaming. "You got to come back when the bears are around, and hear them sons-a-bitches when they are coming at one another."

"Sure," I say, and I think, *Most certainly. No.*

Peacock jams the cork into the scotch bottle.

"You think about it," he says. "It'll do you more good than anything. That roaring will chill your piss. On a warm night."

I'm thinking about being out there alone with God and the grizzly bear, on some tangled hillside right after sunset, and those bears coming at one another. . . . Sure.

LISTENING TO PEACOCK, I find myself drawn to his forthright love of the animal and the wilderness untamed by even so much as backpacker paths, and yet . . . how about that implacable denizen of the bad dreams, the killer in the night?

Such a tangle of feelings toward the grizzly is nothing new. On October 20, 1804, near what is now the border between the Dakotas, along the Missouri River, the Lewis and Clark party ". . . wounded a white bear, and saw some tracks of those animals which are twice as large as the tracks of a man."

So the first recorded wounding came with the first recorded contact by our first scientific foray into the Far West, the beginnings of the cataloguing and grid survey, the naming of parts. The expedition wintered at Fort Mandan, and it was the following spring, April 29, 1805, just upstream from the place where the Yellowstone empties into the Missouri, near the border between Montana and the Dakotas, that the next substantial and legendary encounter took place.

He attacks rather than avoids a man, and such
is the terror he inspires, that the Indians who go in
quest of him paint themselves and perform all the
superstitious rites customary when they make war
on a neighboring nation.

Hitherto those we had seen did not seem desirous
of encountering us, but although to a skillful rifle-
man the danger is very much diminished, yet the
white bear is a terrible animal. On approaching
these two, both Captain Lewis and the hunter fired,
and each wounded a bear. One of them made his escape. The other turned on Captain Lewis and pursued him seventy or eighty yards, but being badly
wounded he could not run so fast as to prevent him
from reloading his piece . . . and a third shot from
the hunter brought him to the ground. He was a
male not quite full grown and weighed about 300
pounds. Its legs were somewhat longer than those
of a black bear, and the talons and tusks were much
larger and stronger. . . . Add to that, it is a more furi-
ous animal, and remarkable for the wounds it will
bear without dying.

*A neighboring nation . . . remarkable for the wounds it
will bear without dying.*

The Lewis and Clark expedition traveled 7,689 miles between May of 1804 and September of 1806. On the way they
discovered 122 animal species or sub-species. The only one
deemed truly dangerous was the grizzly.

By 1890, the last grizzly was killed on the plains. In California, which once had the greatest population of grizzlies,
the mighty golden bear was killed out by 1922. They were
gone from Utah by 1923, from Arizona by 1930, and from
New Mexico by 1931. A female was killed in the San Juan

Mountains of southern Colorado in 1979, the first sighted that far south in thirty years. No trace of others has been found.

It was in 1832, up the Missouri at Fort Union, painting the Mandan Indians—who were to be killed out by smallpox within ten years—that George Catlin saw what was happening. He imagined saving some of it, ". . . a beautiful and thrilling specimen. . . . A Nation's Park, containing man and beast, in all the wild and freshness of their nature's beauty."

On March 1, 1872, Yellowstone Park, 2,221,773 acres, was established by Congress as a public "pleasuring-ground" for "the preservation, from injury or spoilage, of all timber, mineral deposits, natural curiosities, or wonders within . . . and their retention in their natural condition." Glacier National Park was established on May 11, 1910, with essentially the same mandate. Some of our great wild country has been saved. And some of our grizzlies. Today the grizzly occupies only one percent of its original habitat below the Canadian border.

Probably, even by 1916, when Congress established the National Park Service, nobody sensed in any clear way the knife of contradiction implicit in the establishment of these parks, the mutually exclusive purposes implied by the words "pleasuring-ground" and "preservation." The parks were eternally caught in some conceptual no-man's-land between zoo and sanctuary. This dichotomy lies at the heart of the sad controversy that exists today over the National Park Service's grizzly policy. The bears cannot be scrutinized in their wilderness without danger.

Doug Peacock knows this to be true. A man of tangled complexity, bearded and thick-shouldered and animated by obsessive fascination with wild country and the grizzly, Peacock operates outside the scientific wildlife-management community, without proper credentials beyond his years of experience with the animals and his driven hatred of any-one who threatens them.

At the same time Peacock is one of the legendary celeb-rities of antidevelopment politics. It started when Ed Ab-bey based his famous character George Hayduke, in *The Monkey-Wrench Gang,* on his friend Peacock. Such renown, while it can open doors, is also a burden. Doug would like to be seen as more than George Hayduke; he would like to be taken more seriously. He wants people to listen when he says the grizzlies must be given their own country to run.

Coming from a childhood colored by what he calls the "saintliness" of his father, a Boy Scout executive, and week-long solitary trips to the Big Two-Hearted Country of the Upper Peninsula, Doug found himself an SDS radical at the University of Michigan, and then a Green Beret medic in Vietnam. He came home wounded in the soul from a bloody ordeal of healing Vietnamese, and for two years, he says, he was pure crazy, unable to talk in any sort of openly respon-sive way with anyone.

His cure came while he was living in a tent in the out-back country of northwestern Wyoming, where he encoun-tered his first grizzly, a great black alpha-dominant male. The indifferent, dignified otherness of the animal touched Peacock in a way that forced his craziness and anger out into the open, where he could see it as something other than a natural condition of life. Peacock focused his energy on the firm idea of helping to save the grizzly, and he began making a film that would reveal the bear as more than the spook-in-the-night killer inhabiting so many of our worst dreams.

Now Peacock is coming from a decade of trailing the bear through Yellowstone in the snow-drifted spring, and Glacier in the berry-feeding season of summer, bushwhack-ing out alone into their country with his cameras. As he stalks about the lookout room where he has lived with his wife, Lisa, these last six summers, shouting when he gets excited, I think back to the lovely footage he showed us in the afternoon: a sow and her cubs at play in a tiny shallow tarn high in these mountains, batting at one another and blowing bubbles and breaking them in their fun, undisturbed in what we may without sentimentality call a necessary wildness—necessary if we are to continue knowing ourselves as more than extensions of our machines.

"Yeah, that's a nice idea," Peacock says when I tell him where my thoughts are running. "But don't get sappy. With the grizzly you're always taking chances. Some old sow may eat me out from the asshole up. But they got a right. It's their country."

In one sequence, filmed in Yellowstone a couple of years ago, a huge yellow bear comes quietly on Peacock, taking him from the blind side, and just stares him down from close up. At least that was what the animal seemed to be doing in the beginning, jaws chomping softly as if contemplating action—but then the bear lowered its eyes and began pawing at clumps of sedge and pretending to eat, looking full into the camera and then away again, as if willing to consider the possibility of not being the dominant animal in that scenario, maybe forced into a nervous behavior resembling the play-acting indifference of junior-high children at a dress-up party staged by adults. That is what Peacock calls displacement behavior: something to do while you back down gracefully.

If that's what it was, backing down. There is no knowing what a bear might be thinking, but it is obvious they are capable of coming to decisions of real complexity. I keep recalling those stone-hard bar-fighter eyes, and then the flickerings of softness, and wondering if the animal *was* backing down. Maybe it was just taking pity.

"How close was that bear?"

"Right there. I was had. I had to step back to focus." Peacock pulls the cork on our bottle of Glenlivet again. "There was nothing to do but keep the camera running."

Peacock stares down into the neck of the bottle, then looks up grinning. "It was the camera," he says. "He was trying to stare down the camera."

PEACOCK SAYS HE'S BEEN CHARGED maybe forty times, and so far never touched. From what he tells me and judging from his film, the bears react to people somewhat as they react to one another, always evaluating social and predator-prey signals and relationships—if you give them a little time and some space.

There is a "critical attack distance," about fifty yards in open country, within which the bear will feel threatened and, by automatic response, attack rather than retreat. Peacock's advice is to let them know you are coming. Otherwise, up close and surprised—big quick trouble.

Out in the backlands, Peacock says, move slowly through the brush, as any animal does. Stop every few yards and listen, like a deer. The grizzly are threatened by no one but man and usually make a great deal of noise, feeding and crashing about in their self-assured way. When you hear them, give them room. Move slowly once they are aware of you. What Peacock does is talk to them, slowly, in a deep voice. Stand tall, do not panic, and if they charge give them time to stop.

If they don't know you are around, climb a tree. Once they spot you, it is too late. They are too close. If they go at you, drop to a fetal position, and do not resist. They'll generally chew at you a little, and give up. You hope.

Most of all, Peacock says, do not strike out and run blindly. Grizzly country is a dumb place to go jogging. You will resemble prey trying to escape, and they will come after you at an impressive rate of speed in rough country—300 yards in 20 seconds, faster than a quarter horse.

A sow with cubs will often come and look you over, primarily because grizzlies suffer poor vision and can't make out a man for what he is at more than a couple of hundred yards. But then, if you don't get between her and her babies, she'll usually back off.

Sometimes they are just cranky, he says, like the sows when they are weaning their young. Often you can get in trouble with young sub-adults, maybe three or four years old, who have been driven from their mothers but have not yet found their place in the world. They suffer stress and adolescent bewilderment and are about as unpredictable as bears get. And in the fall, when most of the berries are gone and the grizzlies are trying to put on a layer of fat for the oncoming winter, when the competition for forage is most intense, the mature bear can be edgily dangerous.

You can feel it, Peacock says. He and Lisa were ten miles away the night Mary Pat Mahoney was killed in the Many Glacier Campground. You could smell danger in the air, Peacock says.

"Ask Lisa," he says.

So I ask Lisa.

"Yeah," she says. "It's true. Craziness."

It was the same in late September of 1980, Peacock says, when Laurence Gordon was killed while camped in the middle of a feeding ground at Elizabeth Lake. Peacock and Lisa were a couple of drainages away. Many of the animals, Peacock says, were nervous that afternoon, quick on the draw. From what I can make of the story, in the various tellings I have heard, that bear, unlike almost all grizzlies, was intent on killing. Maybe it was just quick anger at the intrusion, or the simple prospect of animal protein for dinner, or one individual's vengeance for the endless insult to the species—if you believe, as some do, that some bears have the wit to hate us. Whatever the reason, Laurence Gordon was a dead man from the time he set up his tent.

With the Glenlivet in hand, I step out on the veranda porch and watch the eclipse proceed and wonder whether we all share a taste for such secondhand dangers, something inherited from childhood—boogeymen in the bedroom—and whether that yearning for darkness doesn't contaminate much of our response to the grizzly. And I wonder if we cannot, as Peacock claims, have a true North American wilderness without the great and dangerous and emblematic bear out there feeding on bulbs of blue camas and tubers of yampa, on biscuit-root, pine nuts, and stinking dead-over-winter carrion. I wonder if wilderness must indeed, by definition, be inhabited by some power greater than ourselves.

The wind blows heavily as we settle toward sleep. The Glenlivet is gone and the eclipse wanes. For this night the frog has given up on eating the moon.

IF YOU UNDERSTAND SCIENCE as I have been taught it, as measurement and data and hypotheses and verifiable conclusions, grizzly studies look pretty shaky—with good reason. Belling a grizzly is not exactly like studying the genetics of fruit-fly populations. To study the bear you've got to get your ass out there in the deepest backwoods and take the risk that your object of scrutiny may come rearing from the next berry patch with a pissed-off look in its eye.

There was no remotely sensible way of getting in close and scientific with the grizzly until 1959, when effective tranquilizers and dart guns came on the scene together. Twenty-some years is not much time in the evolution of science, and so far hard data is in short supply. Too many decisions seem to be made on the basis of personal guess-work, informed opinion, but nevertheless, opinion.

In 1959 John and Frank Craighead, brothers, began their work with the grizzly in Yellowstone, trapping and immobilizing and examining more than 600 bears, radio-collaring and monitoring the activities of a few, collecting what is still the largest bank of data on movements, home ranges, food habits, social and denning behavior, age-sex ratios, mortality rates, and other population factors, gener-ally working toward some understanding of the complex re-lationships between men and bears. By the late 1960s the Craigheads felt they had identified about 75 percent of the grizzlies in the Yellowstone ecosystem, estimating the total in 1967 to be 245 bears.

That was the year the big trouble began. In separate inci-dents on the night of August 13, 1967, two 19-year-old women, Michele Koons and Julie Helgesen, suffered horror-movie deaths by grizzly attack. The killings were vividly detailed in a book called *Night of the Grizzly*. One of those women, it is thought, was killed by a bear that had been feeding at an open garbage dump near Granite Park Chalet in Glacier. The dump was closed. For reasons that in retro-spect seem to have been results of bureaucratic panic, of-ficials at Yellowstone decided to close their own dumps, where grizzlies had been feeding for generations.

The Craigheads, who had done most of their trapping near those dumps, recommended that they be closed gradu-ally. They warned that with sudden closure garbage-habituated bears would likely move out into campgrounds, drastically increasing the chances of human-bear confron-tation. Yellowstone officials disagreed and suggested the Craigheads mind their own business. By 1971, the same year the last dumps were shut down, the Craigheads were gone from Yellowstone.

The next year, a grizzly in Yellowstone killed a young camper named Harry Walker. Walker's parents sued the National Park Service in U.S. District Court in California. Despite Park Service claims that Walker had been illegally camped and careless with his garbage, Judge A. Andrew Hauk found for the plaintiffs in 1975 and sharply rebuked the Park Service for ignoring the Craighead predictions. Harry Walker's heirs were awarded $87,417.67 in damages. The judgment was later reversed on courtroom technicalities. Along the way a lot of battle lines were drawn, and grizzly science became inextricably embroiled in politics.

CONFLICTS OVER SCIENTIFIC GRIZZLY STUDIES— and the numbers such studies produce—are politically loaded. For instance, populations studies: nobody seems to know how many bears we have in the various ecosystems, or whether these populations are on the upswing or decline, or even how many bears it takes to keep a population alive. Answers depend on whom you ask—and to some degree, on why they are guessing.

Clearly it is in the interest of hunters and state fish and game officials, who sell highly valued permits to kill the grizzly, for population estimates to run high. The more bears we have, the more we have for hunters to "harvest." Conservationists and biologists would like to keep population estimates on the low side. An endangered species, after all, tends to generate grant money—more studies, employing more biologists, more bureaucrats. But without an accurate population count your guess is as good as anybody's.

Through all this scientific uncertainty, the National Park Service must concern itself with a very real conflict: how to preserve the bear, host millions of visitors a year, and keep dangerous confrontations minimal. Meanwhile the troubles get worse.

From 1910, when Glacier was created, through 1955, only one person was injured by a grizzly. As Park use accelerated and backpackers replaced horsepackers, the situation changed drastically. Ten persons were injured between 1956 and 1966. Then, in 1967, the dark "Night of the Grizzly," the deaths of Michele Koons and Julie Helgesen, and, in 1972, Harry Walker, and my friend Mary Pat Mahoney in 1976.

On July 24, 1980, Kim Eberly and Jane Ammerman were killed while camping near the eastern boundary of Glacier, and on September 28, 1980, Laurence Gordon was killed at Elizabeth Lake. Some bears were relocated, others shot.

The Park grizzlies clearly have lost what they may never have had, their so-called "shyness"—fear of man. There is vague talk of weeding out the troublemakers, selecting for shyness—which sounds like genetic nonsense—or just plain teaching them some respect. The bears in the Bob Marshall Wilderness, people say, are hunted each fall, and they don't cause all that trouble. Of course, they haven't been crowded by people, either.

There is talk of shooting the bear with rubber bullets, rock salt, and number-nine bird shot, all kinds of "aversive conditioning." The operative concept is pain, and the bottom line, from what I can gather listening to experts, is that nothing really works, consistently. Different bears react in different ways. A hide full of bird shot may cause some to run for cover, but others may come seeking revenge. The only real deterrent seems to be luck and common sense, and, when all else fails, a .44 magnum pistol.

The solution that looks most promising is the management of people: closing areas and trails and keeping the public and bears away from one another. One thing is sure. If we don't take some pains, there are going to be no more grizzlies in our wilderness.

*The whole shitaree. Gone, by God, and naught to care
savin' some who seen her new . . . .*
— THE BIG SKY

BUD GUTHRIE LIVES alongside the Teton River in central Montana, near where he grew up, and dead center in the country he celebrates in his novel. "I wrote that book," he says, "to show the way people kill the things they most love. Like a child with a kitten, they squeeze it to death."

From Bud's kitchen window you can see close-up the fancy mountains of the Rockies' front, the eastern edge of the Bob Marshall ecosystem, some 3,500,000 acres of wilderness, if you include Glacier Park. And all of it is overthrust country. Already, out on the plains around Bud's house, the seismic testing is pretty much completed. And there continues to be talk of oil and natural gas exploration in the Bob Marshall Wilderness itself. Just a couple of miles south from Bud's house lies the Pine Butte Swamp, most of which is owned by The Nature Conservancy, a private foundation dedicated to the preservation of vital wildlife habitat, in this case territory where the last grizzlies dare to come down from their mountain hideout and onto the plains.

But . . . there is talk that we ought to hire professional hunters and wipe the bears out, slick and clean, and have done with all the wilderness-management problems they create. It wouldn't be a matter of their extinction from the earth. There are thousands in Canada and Alaska.

Our major problem is grizzly habitat. The bears need huge spaces to roam, maybe a hundred square miles for males (Peacock says more), preferably without roads or trails or backpackers with orange tents or industrial activity. The bears seem to react to overcrowding as we do: they lose all sense of themselves and drift into a wild aggressiveness, which is beyond doubt one reason for maulings and blood killings in the National Parks. The grizzly, like us, can find the rewards of civilization to be too much of a good thing.

Up there on Huckleberry Mountain, I couldn't sleep after our night with the eclipse and the Glenlivet—call it informational and emotional overload, not to speak of a narrow bed. As the sky broke light over the peaks of Glacier, I found myself deeply moved by the view from our elevation, off west the lights of Montana, Hungry Horse, and Columbia Falls, and farmsteads along the northern edge of Flathead Lake, and back in the direction of sunrise the soft and misted valleys of the parklands, not an electric light showing: little enough to preserve the wanderings of a great and sacred animal who can teach us, if nothing else, by his power and his dilemma, a little common humility.

Yellowstone in Winter

"AGAIN, LAST NIGHT, the coldest place in the nation was West Yellowstone, Montana." That's a story we hear winter after winter on the nightly news, a kind of weatherperson's joke. It's all most American citizens know about Yellowstone in winter.

Which is no doubt a good thing. Winter protects Yellowstone from the hordes of recreational automobilists and bicyclists and tromping backpackers with their multicolored gear, all the cartoon tourists of summertime. You and me and the kids, and Uncle Ted in his Winnebago, and sister Sue whose eyes are blue, everybody in pursuit of a few sweet moments spent checking out a sacred remnant of what we persist in calling wilderness, even after the highways are built. Maybe two million visitors between mid-May and Labor Day.

And then the crowd goes home, leaving Indian summer for those who live in the northern Rockies year-round. Along about the middle of September the leaves go seriously into the business of turning brilliant color along the Firehole River and the other fishing waters. And the trouts, the wonderful slick-bodied trouts, rainbow and brown and cutthroat and brook, are hungry again in the cooling streams and given to lifting ravenously to suck down an ephemeral bit of feather tied handsomely to a barbless hook.

It should be explained that the hooks are barbless if you are an honorable person and only interested in a spot of morning or evening sport. Some meat-eaters go out equipped with a frying pan and a couple of spuds and an onion, and corn flour mixed with salt and pepper in a little

Baggie. And a lemon. Such persons plan to kill one or more of God's living fish right there on a gravel bar, snap the spine and slit open the tender belly and scatter the guts into the brush for the pleasure of raccoons, and wash the trout body in cold onrushing waters, and cook up in the twilight and eat with their fingers.

But much of the time we are not that way. After all, we are the folk who had the good aesthetic sense to live here year-round in the first place. We simply feel it makes good lifetime karma to live in a place where on the evergreen mountain slopes, by early October, the tamarack turns golden, their needles falling through the perfect clarity of afternoon light to litter the undergrowth along the trails like some detritus from heaven.

If that sounds romantic, excuse me. But it's an old custom, our simpleminded xenophobic glorying in the world we have chosen to inhabit in our West. For good reason. Yellowstone is a sacred place, believe it. And it is sacred for reasons beyond landscape and Old Faithful and even the great waterfall on the Yellowstone River. It is sacred for reasons that have nothing to do with our American pride in having at least tried to save some special part of that fresh green continent our people found and overwhelmed with our cities and automobiles and survey lines. It is sacred because of the ecosystem that survives there.

After the tourists are gone Yellowstone belongs to nature again, to the forests and the fungi and, most visibly, to the great animals. All of whom are sacred. It's the way many of us would have it all the time. Fence off the whole damned works, some people say, and lock the gates. God bless them, the extremists, who would kick out everybody but themselves. And I'd be for it if such measures could save the grizzly, who is to my mind the most sacred of all. But that's to my mind.

The damned old gorgeous, terrible grizzly bear. You walk in country where the grizzly lives and you are alert in an ancient way, let me tell you, and in contact with another old animal who walks inside you every day, trapped and trying to get out. Without the grizzly, on our nature walks, we've got nothing to be afraid of but ourselves.

In fall the grizzlies turn irascible as they ever get, absorbed as they are in the hustle for food, layering on fat for the long dozing winter. But we don't mind their outbursts of self-centered crankiness, most of us here, so long as we don't get hurt. What the hell, we say. You don't tear down the Tetons because some climber fell off and got hurt, or killed.

The seasons here are turning, and the thronging thousands of animals are coming down from the high country. The bull elk are responding to hormones and bugling their echoing long cries through the forests, gathering harems and breeding and rigorously defending their lady friends from violation by weaklings and youth. Soon they will be swimming the icy rivers and heading for their winter feeding grounds, mostly outside the Park, maybe 4,000 of them going south to the National Elk Refuge, near Jackson Hole. Another huge herd of perhaps 15,000 will move north of the Park to the country on the west side of the Yellowstone River, beyond the Tom Miner Basin. The bighorn sheep are undergoing the same trials, the rams sniffing the air for signs of females in estrus and running at each other like football players, head to head in heedless combat, the crashing of their collisions echoing among the rocky peaks.

The mallards and the Canada geese and all the other migratory waterbirds gather into vast clamoring flocks and lift into the gray skies of November, heading south. The trumpeter swan does not migrate and endures winter on such open waters as the outlet of Yellowstone Lake. The beaver stockpiles green saplings into his house for winter food, and the timid tiny pika, down there between the rocks on some scree slope, gathers harvest grass to feed on through the winter.

And those few humans who live in Yellowstone during the months between November and March, the Park winter-keepers, they are drying mushrooms and canning peaches and stockpiling three-gallon tubs of ice cream into their freezers. Envy them. Soon the first heavy snows will come, and the Park will be deserted, and they too will settle in, with *War and Peace* or *Atlas Shrugged* or some rugs to weave.

The snows begin to sift through the branches of the Douglas fir, and the interior of the Park is officially shut off to automobile traffic.

Imagine forty below. It's colder than the temperature inside your freezer, and not uncommon when winter has come down on the Park like the hammer it can be. The first heavy snows roll in from the Pacific in great waves, as though they might go on forever in some inexorable end-of-the-world scenario. The plateau around Yellowstone Lake is over 7,700 feet high, and the snow piles up 5 feet deep on the level. The heavy-browed bison plow along, swinging their heads to sweep away the snow and uncover buried yellow grass. The coyotes prey on tunneling rodents who have come up for air, make predatory moves toward buffalo calves, and study the otters at their fishing, hoping to frighten them away from their catch. It doesn't often work.

The cold is now sometimes terrible, and always there. Wind sculpts the frozen snow, and steam rises from the hot pools. The ice on Yellowstone Lake sings its music of tension, the coyotes answering back on clear nights. Elk wade in the Firehole, which is fed by hot springs, and feed on the aquatic life. This is winter in the high northern Rockies. Things have always been like this, except for the snowmobiles.

My friend, Dave Smith, who was a winterkeeper in Yellowstone for six years, says the Park in winter is like a woman's body, lovely in its undulations and dappled with secret places.

"Living by yourself," he says, "you make a pact with trouble." Which sounds like a way of saying "death." Some simple mistake, like a bad fall on cross-country skis, can kill you very quickly when the daytime temperatures run to twenty below and the night starts to come in out of the east at four in the afternoon.

"But once you've settled your mind," he says, "then you just go out there, and you find the warm places, where some little steam vent comes up from the thermal. The ground is soft, and green things are growing." Which is what he means, I guess, when he talks about secret places.

"Winter," Smith says, "is a time of dreams."

Raven Brought the Light

YELLOW SLICKERS in the boutique heart of Vancouver, gay loners and ruined girls edging toward the early tranquility of dense Sumatran coffee from the gleaming Danish machines, and we are headed down to the sea-bound peninsula of meadow and cedar-tree forest which is Stanley Park.

Standing before the fountain outside the aquarium we contemplate Bill Reid's bronze Haida killer whale. The half-imaginary creature arches above the spraying water in delicately articulated North Coast U-form—a great stylized metal fish guarded by a squalling peacock and free-base children fishing the waters beneath for wishing-pool pennies.

The plaque reads: "SKAANA—known by the Haida to be chief of the world beneath the sea, who from his great house raised the storms of winter and brought calm to the seas of summer. He governed the mystical cycle of the salmon and was keeper of all the ocean's treasure."

ARTISTS ALONG THE NORTHWEST COAST, working in the compelling forms of the Haida and Tsimshian and Tlingit and Kwakiutl and Westcoast peoples, are enjoying an explosion of World Class Recognition, and Big Bucks. Bill Reid's killer whale is understood as literally invaluable.

We had come hoping this rebirth of native art might stand as an antidote to that boring aesthetic of alienation which is postmodernism: ... pilgrims in the rain, just checking to see if ancient connections could somehow loop over and heal into the disjunctions of High Art. And now we were facing old questions, wondering if Reid's looming creation was the Real Thing or simply another gleaming brass-colored decoration in the lives of a citizenry gone complacent in the run of their New-World luck.

BY NOONTIME WE WERE PART of the handsome dress-up crowd on Granville Island, south of downtown on False Creek, snooping through the riches in one of the world's great public food markets. Thirty-seven kinds of paté, smoked salmon in long steaks, immaculate trays of fan-tailed shrimp, and glazed papaya. Bill Reid's studio was just along a thronging tourist street, with a display of pleasure-boats beyond.

Reid is the most influential Native American artist on the Northwest Coast. It is justifiable to think of him as the first true master of the North Coast renaissance. Many say Reid began the flowering single-handedly in the 1950s. There were other master carvers still at work—most notably the Kwakiutl artists Mungo Martin at the Provincial Museum in Victoria and Willie Seaweed of Blunden Harbor—but it is clearly sensible to guess that native carving was a dying tradition.

Escaping a career as a CBC radio broadcaster, Reid began his work as an apprentice jeweler in Toronto. "Making pretty baubles," as he puts it, "and learning design."

"But my mother was Haida," he says, "from Skidegate. Before long I was studying the forms, hunting through museums and private collections. My training in design gave me one thing. I knew legends won't help you make art. The story is simply something to depict." Others disagree.

In any event, Reid took his art to a marketplace beyond museums and the tourist trade. In a hard time he showed other North Coast artists the route to financial independence without compromise. "It takes money," Reid says, and he smiles his slow smile. "Money for the artists." He seems to mean freedom.

Bill Reid suffers the terrible shuffling frailty of Parkinson's disease. But he carries on, with irascible humor and considerable help from his friends, many of them once his apprentices, and proceeds steadily with the work of designing and overseeing the production of a monumental piece of Public Art every few years. Such art is understood to spring from the interplay of individual genius and a vision rooted in tradition. "Think," my traveling companion said, "of cathedrals."

Reid's massive sculpture in glowing yellow cedar, "Raven and the First Men," which sits in a special viewing rotunda in the Museum of Anthropology at the University of British Columbia, has been called a "holy masterwork." Reid seems to think such talk is nonsense.

"It's good work," he says, waving his hand to dismiss adulation, and perhaps a certain amount of controversy. "Raven and the First Men" is an ambitious creation that edges out of mythology toward realism, a depiction of that first stunning instant when men emerged from animal consciousness into mindfulness of themselves as fearfully mortal in the world.

"The public is way ahead of the academics," he says. "They recognize art." He tells of children coming to his studio during the days when he and his apprentices were building models of the great Haida whale. "They danced around and loved it," he says. I think of the clamoring children fishing for pennies in that fountain with his bronze killer whale gleaming above them in the rain, and envy this crippled artist the powerful gift he has given his community: pride. Then he shows us a ceremonial ebony-handled knife he is making as a gift for Robert Davidson, who was once his apprentice.

"Robert," he says, "outbid us on that pole for Toronto." And he smiles with what seems to be pleasure in the game he mostly invented, and seats himself at a desk where he works silver, and in his shaking way begins buffing at a tiny replica of the whale, which will be sold exclusively in an uptown gallery, breathing softly on his work and gone away.

ROBERT DAVIDSON IS THE heir apparent, the young master, a consummate craftsman and brilliant designer. Davidson will soon have work on permanent display in the Sculpture Garden in Purchase, New York, alongside Calder and David Smith and Rodin and Giacometti and Noguchi and Maillol. Major work such as the interrelated set of three "watchman" poles that Davidson recently carved for an enclosed mall in Toronto can cost around a quarter-million.

Davidson grew up helping his father, Claude Davidson, carving for the tourist trade in the Haida village of Masset on the Queen Charlotte Islands, deep in an old dark history of heedless imperialism.

The fur traders came first, then the military and the missionaries, and disease. In the spring of 1862, when smallpox struck, there were 8,000 Haida living in some twenty villages. By fall about 500 remained alive. The survivors, who must have been so profoundly stunned by the reeking death of all that was humanly meaningful, moved to the trading centers of Skidegate and Masset, and over to the mainland, where they worked in the salmon canneries on the Skeena River.

By 1900 the few remaining artists were hammering gold and silver coins into bracelets for export to the cities, and were carving the soft black argillite stone found on Graham Island into elaborate smoking pipes and miniature totem poles. Twenty-five cents an inch was the standard price for such work in the years before World War I. A master carver, such as Davidson's grandfather, Charles Edenshaw, did his work for six bits a week. A verified Edenshaw is considered beyond price these days.

Robert Davidson is at that strange and troubling break-over point some lucky artists suffer when it becomes clear they are having a significant career, and not just fooling around in the art world. Among his friends, the artists he began with close to twenty years ago, his is the great distancing success.

"It's like a wave," he says softly, talking about his sense of assurance within his work as we sit over coffee in the kitchen of the immaculate cedar-plank house where he lives outside Vancouver, beyond the suburbs in the rolling farm-land foothills. "It's always moving, never stops. It's always changing. Your feelings and experience come together, and they give you the freedom of confidence in your knowledge. So you just ride it." He looks up a little startled and boyish, as if mystified by the twists of good luck and judgment that have brought him to such pronouncements.

"Ours has always been a public art," he says. "There's tradition, which is the place to start. Our art has to have balance. It has to honor the old and deaths and the fears and sadnesses, and still be part of the mystery and blessedness. It's all there in the people, still alive. You have to go back, into the culture. The work is nothing without the singing and the dancing, where it started."

AIRLINE TICKETS to romantic places. We rode a 727 north to Prince Rupert, drove a rental car up the Skeena River to Tsimshian villages around Hazelton, and flew in a float plane to the Queen Charlotte Islands, all in the interest of going to find the Real Community.

Those old people had lived mainly from the water in their maze of islands and fiords, gathering salmon from their nets and traps in the rivers each spring, enormous spawning runs that never failed and made them rich, the only nonagricultural people in native North America with a continuous surplus of food.

"We got our protein easy," a Haida carver in the village of Skidegate told me, explaining reasons for the elaborate intricacy of their culture. "So we had time to be somebody."

And make war on one another, and take slaves, and— like rich people everywhere, since the invention of settled communities—cultivate a deep interest in the prerogatives of wealth: independence and pride and power and prestige. In wintertime, while rain fell constantly to the breaking seas, they lived an indoor life, secure in huge cedar-plank houses built just above the tide-lines, celebrating themselves and their world with days and weeks of elaborate feasting and dancing.

They understood human life to depend on a healthy and structured natural world, all things alive, the place where they lived inhabited in even its most insignificant aspects, everywhere. And they believed the delicate balance of relationships could only be maintained by ritualized acts of ideal behavior in times of chance or crisis. Out of their collective imagination evolved a resplendent art, stylized and yet individual, nothing naïve or unschooled about it, and inseparable from life because it was always instrumental.

OUR INITIATION into the difficulties inherent in reconnecting with that old reality began on a splendid morning in the Queen Charlotte Islands, traveling by sea-going raft to the long-abandoned Haida village site of Skeedans. Wisps of fog hung in the sunlight between us and the forested mountains, which rose so abruptly to snowy peaks, and our glassy arm of the ocean reflected the world back to us with perfect clarity. By midmorning we were drifting among a cluster of rocky islands maybe a mile out to sea from Skeedans, photographing sea lions and smelling their powerful stench and listening to them roar as they discovered our strangeness.

The young woman who took us, Mary Morse of Kallahin Expeditions, a biologist by training and a bird watcher by avocation, kicked out the clutch on our outboard as we cruised around the rocky natural breakwater toward the tiny crescent of beach at Skeedans. "Well, now," she said, smiling with soft irony, as if she didn't know how to help us with what was coming next. "Ready for the ultimate North Coast experience?"

Sure. Why not? She revved the engine, and we headed in to a place we were only going to be capable of experiencing within the prisms of memory.

Skeedans comes at you slowly. Back amid the trees a few silvery decaying memorial and burial poles were leaning haphazardly, this way and that. Nothing else, right off.

As any traveler would, we stood high on the beach and gazed across the glittering water to other islands where the Haida had lived as lords of the sea—imagining other villages, of the Kwakiutl and Tsimshian and Tlingit—trying to breathe some feeling for what it could have been like to have been Native in that lost time before the Europeans came in their sailing ships, with their cargos of steel carving tools and buttons and sewing machines.

The Russian fur traders who arrived at Sitka in the beginning of the nineteenth century had learned to see in a tradition of iconographic religious art. They quickly recognized that the Natives were artists of a most medieval and compelling kind. Even common household items, such as the spoons made of goat horn, were incised with complex transformational forms.

In the far northern Tlingit villages, women spent a year

spinning and dying and weaving a combination of cedar bark and goat hair into a single magnificently abstract Chilkat blanket, to be worn by a chief in ceremonial glory. Those blankets are among the world's great works of art. And the Russians knew a good thing.

So they traded for the blankets, and the raven rattles whose sculpted images—the prostrate human, the connection of tongues between some creature and man—suggested that any sharing of power was ultimately sexual. And they traded for the masks that literally took the wearer through metamorphosis into another being—Thunderbird or Bear or Wolf: shifting forms emblematic of magical mutuality between men and nature.

The great exodus of holy masterworks began there, first to museums and private collections in St. Petersburg and Moscow, and then to London and Ottawa and the Smithsonian and the American Museum of Natural History. After villages such as Skeedans were abandoned it was a simple thing for private sailing vessels to make away with a few sawed-off totem poles, later to be re-erected on some baronial lawn in Germany or Los Angeles.

THE GREAT-EYED RAVEN and eagle poles with their killer whales and their beaver and bear and frogs and their small human figures, totemically emblematic of legendary animal hierarchies and intimate family histories—they stood gazing out to the turn of seasons from empty villages. The poles had always been allowed to fall and rot when their time came after a century or so. Now the ravens chattered and no children talked back.

At Skeedans we stepped around the mossy timbers that remained from the huge beams of houses where several related families had lived through centuries of building and rebuilding. We discovered human skulls in a shell of a fallen burial pole, both the decaying figures on the pole and the human skulls covered with vivid green moss. We traced the old village house by house and tried to imagine the lives of generations, children running the beaches and slaves at their tasks and the old people dying in a place where they had always lived, at the center of the known world. But we never got beyond our guilty pleasure in the bright beauty of the day and place . . . tourists depicting history, we could never inhabit that old life, or participate in its loss.

On the ride home across the choppy water, the little rhinoceros auklets sprinting to flight before us from the sea and the omnipresent eagles circling out and then back toward their nesting trees on the edges of steep eroding swatches of clear-cut logging, we were stunned from our day on the water, and knew only that we had been privileged beyond our ability to find any response more appropriate than silence.

A WEEKEND LATER, on northern Vancouver Island, we encountered the reborning culture of the Kwakiutl—an imperious people, their potlatch giving the most extravagant on the North Coast, and their art the most baroque. At Alert Bay we found Gloria Webster wearing a badge that read "Survivor."

The U'mista Cultural Center, where she is curator, was built to house a collection of masks confiscated at a potlatch thrown in 1921 by her grandfather, Dan Cranmer. The ceremonies, considered foolishly wasteful and idolatrous, had been going on in secret after being banned by the government in 1884. The masks display a reach of imagination that might frighten any missionary bureaucracy. After a long legal struggle they were returned to the Kwakiutl in 1980.

"We are dedicated to strengthening our people," she

says. At the U'mista Center they are taping old people as they tell tribal stories, and holding native language and traditional dancing classes for children. And making films.

"We have what are called 'aboriginal rights,'" Gloria Webster says. "We are going to use them to prevent destruction of the place where we live. The traditions can come back." A poster on the wall reads: "Potlatch: A Strict Law Bids Us Dance." Well, hell yes, as we say out West. Okay.

ENDURING APPRENTICESHIP TRADITIONS within the North Coast cultures is the factor perhaps most accountable for keeping their arts alive. Charles Edenshaw was the grandfather of Robert Davidson. Doug Cranmer, the grandson of Dan Cranmer, and Gloria Webster's brother, is an important experimental artist. But the most powerful of these lineages runs through the Hunt family, Kwakiutl artists from Fort Rupert, just a few miles up the coast from Alert Bay.

In the dark times, eighty or so years ago, George Hunt was the principal Kwakiutl informant for anthropologist George Boaz and photographer/filmmaker Edward Curtis. And Charlie James was a master carver. James trained his son-in-law, Mungo Martin, a central figure in the survival of North Coast art. Martin ended his career in charge of replicating and restoring poles for the Provincial Museum in Victoria, a vital program of government patronage and training that continues today. Before his death in 1962 Martin trained his son-in-law, Henry Hunt, son of the aforementioned George Hunt, who trained his own son—Tony Hunt, whom we found in his highly successful Arts of the Raven gallery in downtown Victoria.

The prime inheritor of these commingling bloodlines, and an artist of international reputation, Hunt has been another major force in the contemporary renaissance. The

workshop run in connection with his gallery has been training ground for dozens of artists, and the gallery has been a
breakthrough sales outlet for fine work from all over the
North Coast. "Some people are jealous of Tony," one artist
told me. "But lots of them are able to live off their work because of the prices Tony gets."

Hunt works mostly on commissions—$5,000 to $10,000
for a mask, $30,000 to $50,000 for a totem pole. "Our artists
were always for hire," he says. "That's the tradition. From
the old days." Tony Hunt handles the beautiful work in his
shop with the authority of his success and tells us of trips to
Germany and Venezuela and Japan . . . before he drifts into
describing the ceremonial longhouse his family is building
at Fort Rupert, and his eyes at last soften and shine with
pride.

DAYLIGHT WAS OWNED by a man who kept its power
confined in a box until Raven conspired to trick him, steal
the box away, and rescue the Sun. People say Raven released the Daylight, so morning could dawn.

So goes the story of another artist bringing illumination
from the old bag of mysteries. The people say such revela-
tions are sacred.

"Things we don't own are being sold and degraded," Ron
Hamilton says, resting back barefoot and shirtless on a
ragged paint-splotched couch. "Once our sacred images are
flooded onto the world they are dead. Our culture is not a
toy, but many people are selling it into profane situations.
People want you to dance around shopping centers and
look *real Indian.*"

Hamilton purses his mouth with disdain. He is another
major talent, and he has kept his life a long metaphoric
reach from the empire cities, living deliberately in a plain
frame house amid weedy vacant lots on the tribal reserve

in the logging town of Port Alberni, on Vancouver Island, and working only to produce traditional Westcoast screen murals and songs for tribal ceremonies. He does not sell his work, nor much like to have it photographed. "This stuff doesn't mean anything without the ceremonies," he says. "It's only props."

Others of his generation agree, however uneasily. So much has been lost and bought out, and it would be so easy to sell the remnants. The power of success, and the money, call it freedom again, is sweet, and yet . . . I think of Dempsy Bob, an artist of Tsimshian/Talhatan origins, living in Prince Rupert, and a wonderfully gifted carver of ceremonial masks.

Dempsy led us to the cramped apartment bedroom that is his workplace, smiled his anxious selling smile, showed us his new prints and the masks he was working on, and only started to come alive when he took one of his half-finished fantastical yellow-cedar faces into his hands, and began etching it with a curved steel tool, another dreamer gone away into his work. After a long moment he looked up to rediscover us. "I know these boys are finished," he said, "when they start looking back at me."

"IT'S A SIMPLE THING," Ron Hamilton said. "We don't want our children born into an empty place. We want them to feel they have been given a way to live in the world. It's out there in the villages. We have to stay in contact with the old life. Or we don't mean anything." I remembered driving inland along the Skeena River—imagine the Hudson flowing through an endless succession of mountains like those in Glacier Park, snow water falling hundreds of feet from basalt cliffs and roses in bloom down among the cottonwoods—and coming in late afternoon to the ramshackle village that remains at the old site of Kitwancool.

A bronze sign erected by the BC Provincial Government proclaimed "fine examples of primitive art." The poles behind it were about as primitive as Picasso. Standing before a pole named "Hole in the Sky"—metaphor for a cosmic passageway between our house and that of the dead—I felt as distanced as I had at Skeedans.

But then a young boy rode down the gravel road on a tricycle, shrilling hard on a police whistle, and I turned to see a young couple embracing in the open doorway to their home, the low sun illuminating the leaves of springtime aspen by the creek and glowing brassy off snow on the mountains. In the enclosure of that warm evening I was closer to the edges of what we were looking for than I had been willing to let myself imagine.

THERE THEY ARE, hard-handed riders just topping the ridge beyond the arroyo. Squint and shade your eyes against the desert glare, watch them move with quiet assurance, and thrill to their presence. Imagine the harsh clacking mechanical sounds as they lever shells into the firing chamber. Pretty soon now, as we know, they will come riding in and kill to save us from strangers.

It's an old, smoked, and seasoned American scenario: rescue by heroes comes from our wilderness, cowboys and mountain men, Shane and George S. Patton, Big John Wayne from the Monument Valley, Deerslayer after Deerslayer defending us from strangeness and dark tides, bad dreams, savages, and bankers. Our sweet farmstead family-centered life will last forever, so the implications go, if we simply trust in such horsemen to defend our property and virtue.

Heroes are an ancient problem. There is the cutting quickness of violence, the warfare so elementally ended, and then what? The good hero, Shane, rides away into the mystical Tetons and is never heard of again. Who was that masked man? Why did he leave this silver bullet?

MOST OF THE SPECIES we are talking about live in a racist, sexist, imperialist ideological framework of mythology as old as settlements and invading armies. It is important to understand that the mythology of the American West is also the primary mythology of our nation and part of a much older world mythology, that of lawbringing.

Which means it is a mythology of conquest. In America, this secular vision went most public in a story called the Western.

The plot line was there in the early vernacular tales about the possibilities of freeholding and Daniel Boone leading yeoman farmers to conquer the Kentucky outback. It became self-conscious in the novels of James Fenimore Cooper, and was knocked indelibly into our national brains and souls by the oceanic thousands of popular pulp novels published in the last century by such outfits as Beadle's Dime Library. Think of it—1,700 novels about Buffalo Bill and his buffalo killing. It's true.

MOST RUDIMENTARILY, our story of law-bringing is a story of takeover and dominance, ruling and controlling, especially by strength. Our American version springs from a vision of the New World, the vast continent we found, natural and almost magically alive, capable of inspiring us to awe and reverence, and yet curled dangerously around a heart of darkness inhabited by savages.

A disenfranchised pastoral people came to this land from Europe, intent on establishing a civilization where all men were free and equal, and where any man could find and own property. The first problem was the damned Indians. They were already settled on the land, and they wanted to live as they always had, and they had laws of their own to respect. And our law did not always command much respect even from those who brought it: people seeking frontiers are often people seeking escape from law, bringing terrible demons with them—lust and greed, for property and power.

Historically, we know what happened. Our pastoral people killed and they kicked ass, they subjugated the Indians and they took the land, they plundered; and when the dust had settled they owned all things from sea to shining sea, forever. Gold. Water. Whatever.

But the Western, our enfranchising myth, tells a prettier story. In the classical version, a good magical warrior comes from outside society, the terrible land of freedom that exists beyond the law. He is an "outlaw," and because of his life in the wilderness he possesses two skills that have been given up by those who choose to live protected and constrained by law: magical speed of hand with guns, and the wilderness knowledge that it is sometimes necessary to kill in the name of goodness.

This hero saves our people from the savage forces of lust and greed. He alone has the magic and the strength of character to do so. And he is sad because he has to go away after he is finished with the killing, back to the mythological wilderness. His willingness to embrace violence, even in the service of law, is a disruptive force in a society that cannot endorse his ways. He is a killer; he does our dirty work, then carries our social guilt away with him, leaving us to go about the empire-building work of our days with clean hands and souls.

This is our great paradoxical, problematic American teaching story. It is also the plot of *Shane*. The holy and innocent hero comes from the wilderness and slays the dragon, then rides away like a movie star. It is the Western, a morality play that was never much acted out anywhere in the so-called Real West. Or anywhere else.

The actual West was bloody enough, but its inhabitants were never so obsessed with showdown gunfighting as our story would have us believe. Had they been, nobody would have been left alive. More people have been killed in Missoula in any recent year than in Dodge City in its heyday. Certainly the West was not much traveled by holy gunfighters engaged in the business of setting things right.

SO THE YEOMAN FARMERS are saved from the men of greed who covet their hard-earned agricultural land, and Shane, however wounded, must ride back to his mythological home in the Tetons, those most American, isolated, and upreaching mountains. The holy outsider leaves his silver bullet behind in a morality play that excuses us our history of violence. No wonder we loved it—and yet Western movies, by all Hollywood evidence, are dead.

But are they, really?

Why would they be dead? Violence is everywhere, and guilt, and we all want excuses from school. Maybe it's just that our heroes got sick of horses and no sex, riding away gut-shot into the Tetons, and went to other movies.

The Western's so-called demise was already apparent in *High Noon,* which came out in 1952, the year before *Shane.* At the end of a long day, the town saved and the bad men dead in the streets, Gary Cooper looks with contempt on the weak mercantilist townspeople he has defended, who will not move to defend themselves, and he throws his badge down in the dust. Then he rides away in the buggy with Grace Kelly, the Quaker wife who has spent this day learning to respect his warrior skills. Sometimes it is necessary to kill.

A nice Cold-War parable, in which the good society has lost its nerve. By *Bonnie and Clyde,* in the mid-sixties, the heroes had become true professional outlaws, and who could blame them? The good society had become a nasty Great Depression joke in which the rich get richer and the poor suck whatever tit they can find for thin watery sustenance indeed. Despite obscure sexual problems, Bonnie and Clyde fight the bad rich people, and like Robin Hood they return money and pride to the last remnants of the good society, the poor folks back on the farm.

From *Bonnie and Clyde* it was an easy step to the classical professional Western, with its outlaw heroes who live outside society. We were losing face in Vietnam, Manifest Destiny gone loco with napalm, and our nation's children were ducking the draft, smoking dope, and dropping out. Anybody worth a damn was an outlaw, and they were everywhere, the last best hope of humankind gone renegade.

Our good society was deep into chickenshit venality, and everything was upside down. All our ideological chickens were coming home to roost, and we were learning to despise ourselves. The TV news continually played on images designed to generate national self-loathing. Our heroes were left stranded, without a good society to defend. So they banded together and went on alone. *The Wild Bunch* came out in 1969, the same year as *Butch Cassidy and the Sundance Kid.*

Aside from an oasis village of fiercely independent Indians living humanely with one another down in nontechnological Mexico, remnants of a lost life to be yearned for, the only good society was Peckinpah's Wild Bunch itself, a little band of heroic comrades living off the detritus of a culture in which notions of communal life were sunk far into a quicksand of commonplace money-grubbing treachery. Who could care if they killed a whole shitload of townspeople in a street war with the Pinkertons? The classical Western, with strong and independent men defending a good but passive society, had gone away and left nothing worth defending. Butch and Sundance confront an impervious bank safe, mechanically tuned and sophisticated beyond any threat from their six-gun magic, and leave for Bolivia. Freeze frame.

A few years later, John Wayne played a loving old man's eulogy for his life and genre in *The Shootist,* and that seemed the ultimate tip of the cowboy hat. *Adios,* Buckaroo. The hero was gone, and private citizens were left to their own devices, like Charles Bronson in that climax re-venger's comedy, *Death Wish* (1974).

We knew it couldn't be true.

And sure enough, there in the last good movie we could possibly identify as a Western, a movie about a war over California water, Jack Nicholson played our hero resur-rected on the streets of Los Angeles, wisecracking as he leads us down through the circles of urban hell and irony, our own sweet Virgil, until the bottom falls out. It's *China-town* (1974), Jake, where our man is left isolated without the solace of love or respect or even meaningful comrades, and it's hard to think where to turn from his defeat.

Adios, indeed, it seemed to say. Where's that opium? Our society had grown up believing in heroes who would come riding in to save us, and now we found ourselves in a society that wasn't worth saving. Our mythological story was re-vealed as a horseshit excuse for bad conduct and the pursuit of greed, for ruling and controlling, especially by strength.

What we did was wait ruefully for some new mythic flowering from the fire of our troubles, uneasily hanging on to that remnant of the story that says it is at least okay to defend ourselves. Paranoia movies—*Taxi Driver* (1976), *Death Wish* (1974)—had us rooting for random revenge. *Dirty Harry* (1971) nursed the same grudge.

But vigilantism is an uncivilized solution. There are other ways to go. In *48 Hrs.* (1982) a clean, well-lighted black man comes out of the penitentiary wielding the fastest mouth in America and saves our thick-sliced white man's bacon. Our city-hero, the detective whose investigations lead us through to insights about our underworld thickets, has gone Third-World and criminal and hip. Wouldn't it be pretty to think of this film as the cutting edge of possibility— the justifiably embittered grandchildren of slaves and na-tives emerging from the disenfranchised masses to forgive and save us with hard wisdom learned in their downtown wilderness, the story carrying wonderful implications about common humanity in our fight against chaos? Tonto, now that the masked man is gone, did he leave you any of those silver bullets?

It looked like we might have stranded ourselves far enough out on the shores of killer nihilism to be finally driven toward accepting responsibility for our own troubles. Some such recognition as this, however dim, probably accounted for the surprising popularity of a film like *Gandhi* (1982). Confronted with end-of-the-world dragons of our own making, we were finally willing to embrace a hero of decency, whose main weapons were strength of will, intelligence, and *refusal* of heroism as we have known the disease. His gun was his mind, and he used it to back down the whole imperialist British Empire.

But no. We went on to *Rambo* (1985).

In the meantime, back at the ranch, most of our heroes had run away to deep space and comic books. *Star Wars* (1977) played out all the old Western movie stops, magical warriors battling the Empire of merciless technology over nothing specific, Luke Skywalker, armed only with the Force, shutting down his computer to go at the Death Star after Han Solo, the mercenary warrior, couldn't get the job done. Shane saves the Wild Bunch. But since nobody asked us to think the story had any validity beyond diversion we loved it again, and why not?

Didn't it seem right? Escape was what we were looking for, from our powerlessness in the paranoid land of Godfathers, and wasn't it bound to lie out there in the timeless, mythic lands of make-believe films like *Conan* (1982), *Flash Gordon* (1980), *Superman* (1978), and that Punk-Mystic-Western series that started with *Mad Max* (1979)? In those other countries our heroes could still go about their

violent work without anybody having to worry about iden-
tifying with the losers: those people our parents never warned
us about, ourselves.

For weren't daily walking-the-streets moral decisions
complex and ambiguous enough without our having to con-
tend with films like *Breaker Morant* (1980), where the warrior heroes were mercilessly executed by the state after their
time of usefulness ran out? How much did we want to know
about the sadness of heroism and the deeper sadness of our
own yearning for such figures?

AROUND 1953, WHEN I WAS an enlisted man in the Air
Force stationed at Travis, just north of San Francisco, the
little movie house next to the base ran for six months filled
up with crowds for *Shane*. But a few years ago when I
taught it in a University of Montana film course, my audience of undergrad sophisticates laughed. And I could see
why. But underneath I was pissed. *The Wild Bunch* (1969)
was coming soon, and I bet them they wouldn't laugh at
Sam Peckinpah. Sure enough, not one snicker.

Obviously, things have changed since *Shane,* since
1953. Mostly it's the sight of ourselves we see reflected
there. Alan Ladd comes riding toward us, clad in his
mountain-man buckskins, wearing his gun, the Tetons at
his back, and he speaks with quiet Southern courtliness,
the individual who travels alone, the lonely man with
rules. Even his shortness doesn't matter because he is just
so damned competent and sure of himself. We know he
yearns to be absolved of his loneliness and don't blame
him for falling in with the family unit of Van Heflin, Jean
Arthur, and Brandon De Wilde, and siding with them and
their agricultural neighbors against the traditional forces
of acquisitiveness, the brutal ruling-class ranchers and
their hired gunfighter, Jack Palance.

Money is always the core of these troubles. Shane is victorious at the end, as we knew he would be. It's a story we responded to with love in 1953. It seems simpleminded and sentimental now.

What has changed? Just us, our sense of what is possible in our society. *The Wild Bunch* tells us no such fairy tales about the possible triumph of pastoral life. The Wild Bunch are criminals rather than mountain men, in search of a last good heist, pursued by one of their own kind, Robert Ryan, another outsider, the only man capable of corralling them. But among themselves they still have a code of conduct. At least they do not lie to one another, and we still respect that remnant of what was dreamed of as America.

In *The Wild Bunch* both Anglo and Mexican societies are irreversibly corrupt. An Anglo drunk gives temperance lectures, and a Mexican general is infatuated with his automobile. But the pastoral dream has not vanished. Hidden in villages there is another life that might survive, although we doubt it, and doubt that it could do so for long. As for the Wild Bunch themselves, they are doomed, and go to their doom with sad relish, recognizing that modern life is impossible for them.

And the final image is not the great ceremonial slaughter we all remember; as the credits come down, it is the Wild Bunch riding out from that pastoral village bathed in green light and song and deep in the heart of the last good time while we wait to be discovered by a new story with which to order our lives, in which the strong inherit the earth for better reasons than firepower.

Doors to Our House

DICK HUGO USED TO SAY certain writers own certain words. The rest of us cannot use those words. Dick was thinking about Gerard Manley Hopkins and *dappled*. Should we use that lovely word, everybody would immediately think, Aha, derivative of Hopkins. It's true.

So, do not write anything about the dappled apples under the light in trees that bear apples. Not even if those apples lie around in the homestead of your memory. No matter what you do, the word *dappled* will ring of Gerard Manley Hopkins.

In the northern West certain writers have built for us a texture of metaphor around *sky—The Big Sky, Wind from an Enemy Sky, This House of Sky*—so it might be said they have found for us a way to claim emotional ownership of the word, and of its implications in our part of the world. Titles are names for whatever books are about, and among other things these books are about infinity and shelter, prospect and refuge, individualism and community. In them, like a set of mirrors, we have come to see ourselves and some of the psychic responsibilities inherent in inhabiting our piece of the earth from a perspective that is useful.

The jolt of recognition so many of us experienced when we first read *The Big Sky* had much to do with that title, and with what the book told us about the difficulties of staying humane when confronted with enormities of actual distances that often look to be unmappable. In the northern West we are always in danger of submitting to the implications of those distances and allowing ourselves the ruinous privilege of believing they are real and inevitable morally as

well as physically. We are always tempted to find the difficulties of maintaining community too burdensome, and
translating our physical isolations into indifference to the
fate of others.

Think of Meriwether Lewis, as he came to the top of
Lemhi Pass, imagining he would see some great highway of
river toward the Pacific, instead confronted with ranges of
mountains feathering off to a dim horizon with that terrifying expanse of sky beyond. It would be easy to see our own
frailties written equally large when contemplating such real
disconnections, and excuse ourselves anything. We might
be tempted toward huddling into our fearfulness, cultivat-
ing the arts of selfishness. *The Big Sky* is among other things
a cautionary tale telling us this temptation is no answer.

In *Wind from an Enemy Sky,* D'Arcy McNickle showed
us the far and even darker side of the same predicament, native communities shattered by the unfathomable imperial-
istic gusts of what is called civilization. When Ivan Doig
entitled his book *This House of Sky* he was taking on big
medicine, reaffirming and at the same time amending notions about the importance of that shelter which is family,
and of the ultimately coherent self that grows out of family.

These are powerful books, and the central metaphor
that helps generate their power—*sky*—is located securely
in place, in region, in Montana and the northern West.
Through the act of finding such a metaphor, and exploring
it, these writers made it a gift to those of us who live here.
We look out to our distances through the lens of that notion
in its complexities, and we see meaning. Through generations of living in this difficult place, with the help of our
artists, we have come to possess resonances that help fill our
silences. This kind of emotional ownership is as close as we
will ever come, really, to owning any place.

The way I see it now is that you either make a little
nation and solve its historical and personal problems
within the format of your own household—accepting
the mistakes that you've made, all the ones your
parents made, all that your children make, and all
the mistakes your country has made—and you win
that one or you lose the only war worth fighting.

Moreover, as soon as you step out of this person-
ally constructed world and, say, drive into town or
stand out on I-90 and watch our nation cycle through
these placeless arteries, it's there that you confront
the true horror of the other option.

— THOMAS MCGUANE,
interviewed in the *Paris Review*

A FEW YEARS AGO the *New York Times Book Review* sent
David Quammen around to interview people and write a
piece about "Montana Writers." In Missoula, some people
got together in the Eastgate Liquor Lounge, as they did in
those days, and Quammen quizzed us about why so many
writers have settled in Montana. Max Crawford, a Texan
who was living in town at the time, said it was because writers needed to live cheap.

"It's like Paris in the 1920s," Max said. "All those writers
talked like it was Paradise, but soon as the exchange rate
dropped they all went home."

A while later, in the *Montana Review of Books,* Bill
Vaughn wondered why—if living cheap was some kind of
criterion—North Dakota wasn't full of writers. You can
live cheap in North Dakota. Vaughn implied that something else was going on.

While never doubting that money is real important, since
it can equal freedom for an artist, I tend to agree with Vaughn.
Writers and other artists are congregating in Montana and

its environs for reasons beyond money—like the possibility of living in the local company of peers, connected to a place knowable in human terms, where you can walk around like a citizen in a recognizable community.

But I can also understand where Max Crawford was coming from. Max was outraged by the idea of being tagged a regional, and therefore a minor, writer. This is where I have trouble. I don't see the conjunction of "regional" and "minor."

What I mean to argue, in fact, is that art has a much greater chance if it starts in a particular place, like Oxford in Mississippi, and moves out toward the Nobel Prize. Think of it this way: we all have our complaints about television and movies, the imperial art of our culture. The run of it is superficial and silly. We wonder if it has to be that way, and if so, why?

The answer seems simple enough. Driven by enormous production and distribution expenses, movies and television must draw huge coast-to-coast audiences if they are to pay their bills. So they tell stories about some homogenized America that does not exist except in dream, a never-never land. It's art designed for the widest possible audience, all of America and the world overseas, and as such it isn't about anybody, really, and it's not centered anywhere actual. How could it speak to any of us in our deepest, most local concerns? There are exceptions, of course, since most good film and TV people are deeply aware of these concerns. But the complaint continues to be valid: our most pervasive art forms are our most superficial.

At the recent Montana History Conference in Helena some people from Fort Peck exhibited and talked about the Star Quilts made by women on the reservation, and people from the college in Pablo on the Flathead Reservation showed us a videotape of a woman doing fine work with deer and elk hides. Those people showed us arts that had evolved in a local place, in response to complex abilities and needs, over generations. The art reflected particular people as they responded to the actualities of their lives and histories, and because of that it was unique and singular— speaking to us of individual relationships to beauty and attempts to define what is sacred. We are moved by such art, when we are moved, because in it we see ourselves striving to make sense of things, continually redefining our notions of what is valuable. Such identification encourages us to be humane.

What I'm trying to say is that regional art is important because it is mostly the only art that is useful in our efforts to know ourselves, even if only locally. And there are times when it transcends its regionality. No art could be more securely located in a particular time and place than *The Iliad* or *Don Quixote* or *Moby-Dick* or Shakespeare or Sophocles or *The Canterbury Tales* or *Remembrance of Things Past.* Or the great wood carving done by Tsimshian and Haida and Tlingit artists along the Northwest Coast of North America. Make your own list: most of the great stuff starts local, rooted in one-of-a-kind lives and communities, maybe Plentywood or some house on a side street in Paris.

~

I have never distinguished readily between thinking and dreaming. I know my life would be much different if I could ever say, This I have learned from my senses, while that I have merely imagined. I will try to tell you the plain truth.

— MARILYNNE ROBINSON, *Housekeeping*

OVER THE LAST FIFTY or sixty years artists in the American West have gone through a long and difficult battle, claiming and reclaiming their emotional homeland. It's fair to say that up until the 1930s most major art set in the American West was centered around the myth of the Western: gunslingers and settlers and savages, invading armies and law bringing.

Not that the myth didn't spring from some actual anecdotes. It's just that our out-West experiences were taken over by storytellers eager to satisfy audiences more interested in romance than in any real story. Even an artist like Charlie Russell, so deeply rooted in the gone-hungry dustiness of daily life in Montana, so concerned about getting each detail right, did not escape.

Russell's paintings for the most part portray the great romance of the Western—strong heedless figures on an enormous, gorgeous landscape. Charlie Russell came west to find adventure, and he painted the adventure he found. It's easy to understand why his work remains so popular in the hometown he found and loved, Great Falls, and all over the West. His paintings tell us our lives are connected to great doings in a grand sweep of mythological story, and significant. Russell saw through the lens of that story and painted what it allowed him to see.

Mark Twain looked to the East, from where the culture came, wrote the silliness of *Roughing It* for an Eastern audience, and then migrated as quickly as he could to New York to celebrate his literary triumph. Buffalo Bill's Wild West Show performed before sellout crowds in Europe, but surely told little of truth or importance. And even early on, some were nettled by the bald nonsense. In Wild Bill Hickock's first stage venture the script called for him to sit by a crêpe-paper campfire, sipping whiskey and spinning yarns. On opening night Hickock took a healthy swig of what proved to be cold tea, spat it onto the boards, and bellowed, "I ain't telling no lies until I get some real whiskey."

The myth has been an insidious trap for those who would write about the American West, a box for the imagination. For a long time it was as if there was only one legitimate story to tell about the West, and that was the mythological story.

William Eastlake once told me to never let a publisher put a picture of a horse on the cover of any novel I might publish. "The people who buy it will think it's some goddamned shoot-up," Eastlake said. "And they'll hate it when it isn't."

Eastlake was saying that Western writers somehow have to insist that the real, emotionally possessed life they grew up inside of, or found when they came to the country—as opposed to the stylized morality play that was supposed to be Western experience—was worth writing about. Many of us have shared the difficulty of working when expected to write from inside myth. But it's not so bad anymore, mostly because of the hard labor of some widely disparate writers we can think of as drawing together under an ungainly label: *antimythological.*

In 1903 Andy Adams published *Log of a Cowboy,* detailing a late nineteenth-century cattle drive from northern Mexico to the Blackfeet Reservation in northern Montana. The story is reasonably accurate and well told, talking of days in the saddle and without drinking water, of dust and cold wind and putting your saddle in a gunnysack at drive's end and taking the train home to Texas. It was a life with no room for the lacy-sleeved mythological six-gun exhibitions of Main Street gamblers.

Willa Cather was born in 1873, grew up in Red Lodge, Nebraska, met Stephen Crane, determined herself on a career in writing, moved to work as an editor in New York for a while, became a lover of women, and eventually took the advice of Sarah Orne Jewett to "find your own quiet center of life and write from that."

It's an old story with American artists. Having gone into

exile in New York or Paris or some far-away land that may exist only in the mind, they find imaginative freedom to look home. Think of Hemingway looking back to Michigan, or Max Crawford in Missoula during the early 1980s, writing his fine, undervalued novel about the history of his home country in west Texas, *Lords of the Plain.* In 1918 Cather published her famous novel of Nebraska life, *My Ántonia.*

Ole Rölvaag was born in Norway, in 1876. At the age of twenty he emigrated to his uncle's farm in South Dakota, went off to school, and at thirty became a teacher at St. Olaf College. At the age of fifty, in 1926, he published his great gone-crazy-in-the-distances story of Norwegian emigrant life on the Dakota plains, *Giants in the Earth.*

By the 1930s, off obscure in the Sand Hills of Nebraska, a girl named Mari Sandoz, likely inspired by the example of Willa Cather and Rölvaag, had matured tough enough on a homestead ranch. She was making ready to write a book about her father—who was one of those damned old litigious autodidact unbathed loons we find all over the West—and the women who kept him functioning. At the end of her story she tells of Jules in his deathbed, finding a newspaper item about a writing contest she had won. As she tells it: "He tore the paper across, ordered a pencil and paper brought, wrote her one line in the old, firm, up-and-down strokes: 'You know I consider artists and writers the maggots of society.'"

Why wouldn't he? Hadn't they told nothing but lies about the strenuous facts of life where he had lived, the turn of endless horizon and the turkey-packed earth where the wash-water was flung outside the backdoor of the ranch house, season after season as the generations passed? Mari Sandoz gives this eulogy:

> Outside the late fall wind swept over the hard-land country of the upper Running Water, tearing at the

low sandy knolls that were the knees of the hills,
shifting, but not changing, the unalterable sameness
of the somnolent land spreading away to the east.

Jules could not know that Mari, like H. L. Davis, John
Steinbeck, Walter van Tilburg Clark, Wallace Stegner,
A. B. Guthrie, Jr., and an assortment of others less well
known, was getting ready to write books that would attempt to convey the emotional truth of the various Western
lives they had lived and witnessed and come to possess
while inhabiting the country. Jules died in 1928.

Old Jules was published in 1935. It ought to be one of the
sacred white-man texts for writers in the modern West. If
you start reading around in journals and diaries and letters
from the early West, mostly written by women, you will find
a quite different story than those written for publication in
the East. For instance, you will hardly ever find a holy gun-
slinger come from the wilderness to right the troubles of society. Instead you will find—how to put it?—the perfect
eccentricities of everyday life, your local and quite detailed
Weather Reports, both sacred and demonic, mental and
otherwise. You will find the so-called "real" life as she was
experienced, snakes, dust, sod-house walls, wash-water and
all. And you will find the same sort of item in *Old Jules:* the
splintery texture of the actual, sanded a little by art, but
there like rocks beneath the water.

Willa Cather and Ole Rölvaag and Mari Sandoz got
away to school and learned some craft, and then went home
to write up the verities they had learned nearby, while they
were at it finding for us in the American West a set of beginnings: what we might think of as a literature springing from
experience, not much like that romantic and nonsensical,
melodramatic morality play which is the Western.

The doors were open; the idea was in the air; and the

good books came, each helping free us to the notion that the specific instances of our lives might be a fit subject, if somebody could manage it, for that old *beau idéal,* high art. Out in Oregon, in 1935, H. L. Davis won the Pulitzer Prize for *Honey in the Horn.* Walter van Tilburg Clark published *The Ox-Bow Incident* in 1940; Wallace Stegner published *The Big Rock Candy Mountain* in 1943; Bud Guthrie published *The Big Sky* in 1947. All this chronology is maybe just the hindsight detailing of what we want to see, but by one means or another the next generations of Western writers have taken heart from it.

Listen to Wallace Stegner, from *The Big Rock Candy Mountain*:

> Things greened up beautifully that June. Rains came up out of the southeast, piling up solidly, moving toward them as slowly and surely as the sun moved, and it was fun to watch them come, the three of them standing in the doorway. When they saw the land to the east of them darken under the rain Bo would say, "Well, doesn't look as if it's going to miss us," and they would jump to shut the windows and bring things in from the yard or clothesline. Then they could stand quietly in the door and watch the rain come, the front of it like a wall and the wind ahead of it stirring up dust, until it reached them and drenched the bare packed earth of the yard, and the ground smoked under its feet, and darkened, and ran in little streams, and they heard the swish of rain on roof and ground and in the air.

And this, from the story "Carrion Spring," in *Wolf Willow:*

> Three days of chinook had uncovered everything that had been under the snow since November. The

yard lay discolored and ugly, gray ash pile, rusted
cans, spilled lignite, bones. The clinkers that had
given them winter footing for the privy and stable
lay in raised gray wafers across the mud; the strung
lariats they had used for lifelines in the blizzard
weather had dried out and sagged to the ground.
Mud was knee-deep down in the corrals by the sod-
roofed stable, the whitewashed logs were yellowed
at the corners from dogs lifting their legs against
them. Sunken drifts around the hay yard were a
reminder of how many times the boys had had to
shovel out there to keep the calves from walking
into the stacks across the top of the snow. Across
the wan and disheveled yard the willows were bare,
and beyond them the floodplain hill was brown.
The sky was roiled with gray cloud.

A generation of writers were proving that the West had
more compelling stories than those of simpleminded gun-
play, that the private lives lived in the West were worth
writing about just as any life is worth art if, in seeing it
through the eyes of the artist, we are helped to see our own
life with renewed clarity.

~

And they never thought they'd have a girl from this
reservation as a saint they'd have to kneel to. But
they'd have me. And I'd be carved in pure gold. With
ruby lips. And my toenails would be little pink ocean
shells, which they would have to stoop down off their
high horses to kiss.

— LOUISE ERDRICH, *Love Medicine*

TRY THIS FOR OPENERS: the art of a region begins to come mature when it is no longer what we think it should be.

Imagine 1929, reading *The Sound and the Fury* in the deep South. How crazy that book must have seemed, how unsettling and unreal, actual. But, if you want a sweeping, oversimplified but partways true generalization, grown-up Southern literature began there. Right away Faulkner was followed by Eudora Welty, Robert Penn Warren, Katherine Anne Porter, Carson McCullers, and Flannery O'Connor.

Clearly, even without a genius like Faulkner to get things started, the same sort of phenomenon is taking place all over the inland reaches of the American West. Back in the middle '70s Dorothy Johnson sent me a book to review for the local newspaper. "I don't know if this is any good," she said. "It's sure got a strange title." She went on to tell me the author was a man who had grown up in Missoula, then gone off to spend his life teaching at the University of Chicago. The book, of course, was *A River Runs Through It.*

And indeed, it seemed pretty strange to me. *In our family there was no clear line between religion and fly fishing.* Now was that any way to start a story set in the West? About halfway through the news began to sink in.

This was not just some odd set of memories written down by an old man. This was the real goddamned thing, Literature, and the climactic events took place alongside a fishing hole where I had been skunked only the week before. In retrospect, that was when I first began to suspect the West was going to have itself an adult literature. I mean, there had been some terrific books in recent years, *House Made of Dawn, Desert Solitaire, The Milagro Beanfield War, Ceremony, Winter in the Blood,* Dick Hugo—but for me it was Maclean, so quirky and rock-solid and unexpected, who pointed out that the doors of possibility were open wide.

Sometimes it is a comfort to believe that one day is
like another, that things happen over and over and
are the same. But accidents happen, and sometimes
a man or a woman is lucky enough to see that all of
it, from the first light kiss onward, could have gone
another way.
— DAVID LONG, *Home Fires*

SO, OUT IN OUR WEST, artists are trying to run their eyes
clear of mythic and legendary cobwebs, and see straight to
the actual. But sometimes you have to wonder about that.
As a friend of mine says, "I ask for truth, and what do I get?
Candor."

You have to suspect that much of the attraction of Evan
Connell's big-selling Custer book, *Son of Morning Star,*
comes from its willingness to tell anything, the sense it con-
veys that this is the real story with blinders off. It's a book
that reeks of atrocious detail, atrocity after atrocity. You
have to stay a little leery of such impulses. Maybe it's truth,
and maybe it's only a chronicle of sensational murdering,
no more meaningful than the front page of the local paper,
with its daily bloodbaths.

Or not. You also have to be edgy about such categoriz-
ing. You run into books like *Blood Meridian* by Cormac
McCarthy, a recent novel about scalp-hunting in the Southwest after the Mexican War, a story so beautiful and vivid
with horror it makes your worst dreams look like popcorn,
and you don't know what to say.

Let it go at this: there is indeed a new candor afoot in the
land. Maybe it's part of the impulse to see straight to the
beating meaningful heart of things, but sometimes it's only
hearts torn apart while we watch: candor, a manifestation
of our nostalgia for the old days when violence seemed
meaningful.

Anyway, it probably all helps clear the decks. For what? Quickly now, we will stagger through a list of my favorites, writers who are coming to maturity in the West, or writing about the West in mature ways, most of them not exactly famous yet: Bill Yellow Robe, Robert Wrigley, Roberta Hill Whiteman, David Long, Douglas Unger, Richard Ford, Sandra Alcosser, David Quammen, Gretel Ehrlich, Patricia Henley, Ralph Beer, Paul Zarzyski, Mary Blew, Marilynne Robinson, Louise Erdrich, Jim Welch, Edward Abbey, Leslie Marmon Silko, Cyra McFadden, Tom McGuane, Elizabeth Tallent, Ivan Doig, John Keeble.

I'm out of breath, and out of faith with this kind of listing. It seemed a good idea while I had the chance, but it doesn't mean much. I apologize to those left off because of my ignorance. Read the work and find your own favorites.

The point is, they come from all over the place, Montana City, Santa Barbara, upstate Wisconsin, the Mississippi Delta, New York City, and live all over the place, few of them much over forty, and they are doing work strange and varied as the country. What if we listen to a few lines from *Love Medicine* by Louise Erdrich, and *Housekeeping* by Marilynne Robinson, novels private and immaculate as the inside of a cat's mouth, and then shut up and think things over? Like this, from *Love Medicine,* set on a reservation in North Dakota:

> Your life feels different on you, once you greet death
> and understand your heart's position. You wear
> your life like a garment from the mission bundle sale
> ever after—lightly because you realize you never
> paid anything for it, cherishing because you know
> you won't come by such a bargain again. Also you
> have the feeling someone wore it before you and
> someone will after.

And this, from *Housekeeping,* set over in Sand Point, Idaho:

> Of my conception I know only what you know of
> yours. It occurred in darkness and I was unconsent-
> ing. I (and that slenderest word is too gross for what
> I was then) walked forever through reachless obliv-
> ion, in the mood of one smelling night-blooming
> flowers, and suddenly—My ravishers left their
> traces in me, male and female, and over months I
> rounded, grew heavy, until the scandal could no
> longer be concealed and oblivion expelled me. But
> this I have in common with all my kind. By some
> bleak alchemy what had been mere unbeing be-
> comes death when life is mingled with it. So they
> seal the door against our returning.

Revenge

WHAT WE WILL DO about the bastard fragility of things is this: we will walk away from the trailhead and labor our fleshy way up over the divide, sweat stinging in the corners of our eyes, and at the summit we will stand and gaze forward into our new land. Far below an empty cattle truck sings toward a destination on the hot asphalt, but we are gone away. The odor of burning diesel is not a thing we can recall with any clarity.

We wash our faces in the mossy spring and stand quiet, gazing up to the peaks where the night's midsummer dust of snowfall is burning away under the noontime sun, and we are no longer soft, or fleshy. Already our hands are hard, the calluses forming.

The man with a red-flowered bandana tied around his forehead turns, and when he smiles his eyes are pale as the sky. He shakes his head, acknowledging the enormous fortune we have come to find, and we gather ourselves to follow his lead, down the trail between snow-stunted fir and into the lower country where the ferns reach to us from amid the yellow pine.

In the meadows where the beaver dammed the creek so long ago, elk are grazing alongside white-tailed deer, and we kill a young buck for camp meat. Just as we settle toward sleep a white owl descends on a long turn through the night over our cooking fire, seemingly unafraid. Already some of the women are making plans for the winter, although the men cannot bring themselves to speak of it. That will come later, when we have reached the open riverside lands where the buffalo winter, and we begin notching logs for our cabins.

With spring the first child will be born, and the wild horses will come from the south of their own accord. The walls of our cabins will be strung with pelts, stretched and drying. Some of the men will volunteer to ride out for cattle and white paint for the fences. They go, and as we had feared, they never return. But the roses we planted before they left have grown lush, and we pray for them in our circle of giant pines, our knees on the soft cushion of needles. We know that such absences are only natural, like the fall of leaves in the autumn afternoons before winter.

And then with the first snowfall, when the tracking is easy, a party returns from hunting with the report that they have sighted a strange horned animal. Its pelt is golden and tinged with gray. The picket gate before the house swings open gently under their hands. They stand uneasily, shifting their feet on the frozen grass. Beyond them the mountains shimmer white under the sun. We wonder at the animal. Perhaps it was sadness. The men leave off their splitting of wood, and the children whimper in their sleep.

It is over. No one but God will ever know where we have gone, and the time is our secret. Sunday we will walk out, and Monday we will punch in. Far back in our eyes there will be a feathery and ironic glow of triumph.

WILLIAM KITTREDGE grew up on and then managed his family's cattle ranch in eastern Oregon. He studied in the Writers' Workshop at the University of Iowa and became the Regents Professor of English and Creative Writing at the University of Montana until retiring in 1997. He has received numerous prestigious awards, including a Stegner Fellowship at Stanford, two Writing Fellowships from the NEA, and two Pacific Northwest Bookseller's Awards for Excellence. He was co-producer of the movie *A River Runs Through It.* Kittredge has published in more than 50 magazines and newspapers, among them the *Atlantic, Harper's, Esquire, Time, Newsweek, TriQuarterly,* the *Paris Review,* the *Washington Post,* the *New York Times,* and the *Los Angeles Times.* His books include *Who Owns The West? A Hole in the Sky, The Nature of Generosity, Taking Care: Thoughts on Storytelling and Belief, The Van Gogh Field,* and *We Are Not in This Together.* With Annick Smith, he edited *The Last Best Place: A Montana Anthology.*

Owning It All has been typeset in Old Style No. 7, a modernized version of the classic Caslon type. It's lineage goes back to a face cut in the middle of the nineteenth century by the Miller and Richard Foundry of Edinburgh, Scotland. That face, in turn, engendered another old-style face cut in the United States by the Bruce Foundry in the 1870s. The version used here was cut by the Linotype Corporation in the 1920s.

Book design by Wendy Holdman.
Typesetting by Stanton Publication Services, Inc.
Manufacturing by Bang Printing on acid-free paper.

Graywolf Press is a not-for-profit, independent press. The books we publish include poetry, literary fiction, essays, and cultural criticism. We are less interested in best-sellers than in talented writers who display a freshness of voice coupled with a distinct vision. We believe these are the very qualities essential to shape a vital and diverse culture.

Thankfully, many of our readers feel the same way. They have shown this through their desire to buy books by Graywolf writers; they have told us this themselves through their e-mail notes and at author events; and they have reinforced their commitment by contributing financial support, in small amounts and in large amounts, and joining the "Friends of Graywolf."

If you enjoyed this book and wish to learn more about Graywolf Press, we invite you to ask your bookseller or librarian about further Graywolf titles; or to contact us for a free catalog; or to visit our award-winning web site that features information about our forthcoming books.

We would also like to invite you to consider joining the hundreds of individuals who are already "Friends of Graywolf" by contributing to our membership program. Individual donations of any size are significant to us: they tell us that you believe that the kind of publishing we do *matters*. Our web site gives you many more details about the benefits you will enjoy as a "Friend of Graywolf"; but if you do not have online access, we urge you to contact us for a copy of our membership brochure.

www.graywolfpress.org

Graywolf Press
2402 University Avenue, Suite 203
Saint Paul, MN 55114
Phone: (651) 641-0077
Fax: (651) 641-0036
E-mail: wolves@graywolfpress.org

Other Graywolf titiles you might enjoy:

The Stars, the Snow, the Fire
  by John Haines

The Way It Is: New & Selected Poems of Willliam Stafford

The Saddest Pleasure: A Journey on Two Rivers
  by Moritz Thomsen

Crossing the Expendable Landscape
  by Bettina Drew